Little Lamb, Who Made Thee?

Other books by Walter Wangerin, Jr.:

Reliving the Passion
Mourning Into Dancing
Branta and the Golden Stone
The Book of the Dun Cow
The Book of Sorrows
The Bible for Children
Ragman and Other Cries of Faith
As For Me and My House
Miz Lil and the Chronicles of Grace

Little Lamb, Who Made Thee?

A Book About Children and Parents

Walter Wangerin, Jr.

ZondervanPublishingHouse
Grand Rapids, Michigan

A Division of HarperCollinsPublishers

Little Lamb, Who Made Thee?
Copyright © 1993 by Walter Wangerin, Jr.

Requests for information should be addressed to:
Zondervan Publishing House
Grand Rapids, Michigan 49530

Library of Congress Cataloging-in-Publication Data

Wangerin, Walter.
    Little lamb, who made thee? : a book about children and parents / Walter
Wangerin, Jr.
        p.   cm.
      ISBN 0-310-40550-5
      1. Parenting—Religious aspects—Christianity. 2. Wangerin, Walter. 3.
Parents—United States—Religious life. I. Title.
    BV4529.W26   1993
    248.8'45—dc20   93-29995
                                                                                            CIP

Published in association with the literary agency of Alive Communications, P.O. Box 49068, Colorado Springs, CO 80949.

Cover design by Gary Gnidovic

Printed in the United States of America

93 94 95 96 97 98 99 00 01 02 / DH / 10 9 8 7 6 5 4 3 2 1

This edition is printed on acid-free paper and meets the American National Standards Institute Z39.48 standard.

Contents

PART IV
THE PARENT, FINALLY, OF HIS PARENTS

The Lamb

Little Lamb, who made thee?
Dost thou know who made thee?
Gave thee life, and bid thee feed
By the stream and o'er the mead;
Gave thee clothing of delight,
Softest clothing, wooly, bright;
Gave thee such a tender voice,
Making all the vales rejoice?
Little Lamb, who made thee?
Dost thou know who made thee?

Little Lamb, I'll tell thee,
Little Lamb, I'll tell thee:
He is calléd by thy name,
For he calls himself a Lamb.
He is meek, and he is mild;
He became a little child.
I a child, and thou a lamb,
We are calléd by his name.
Little Lamb, God bless thee!
Little Lamb, God bless thee!

— From *Songs of Innocence*
by William Blake, 1789

A Note from the Editor

"Unless you turn and become like children, you will never enter the kingdom of heaven"—Matthew 18:3

I don't know whether to be encouraged or worried by Jesus' admonition to become like a child. On one hand, I'm already an overachiever in childishness: I'm good at pouting, showing off, telling white lies, throwing temper tantrums—all perfectly infantile characteristics, which I veneer over, of course, with a thick layer of adult subtlety. On the other hand, it is at those times that I feel farthest from the kingdom of heaven, which leaves me wondering: Just what does Jesus mean?

Before I had answered that question, something happened to me that happens to a lot of us grown-but-still-perplexed children: My wife and I were expecting a child of our own. Prepared or not, we began to make room in our lives for this unimaginable visitor—who, though growing steadily in Shelley's body month after month, seemed so far away, as if arriving slowly from a distant star or another dimension.

To my relief, though, I had an advantage over the other expectant fathers I knew; I had a secret comfort and guide. I was fortunate enough to be editing this book, *Little Lamb, Who Made Thee?* by Walter Wangerin, Jr., a writer I've long admired and have recently come to know personally. The stories in this book prepared my soul for parenthood in a way that no "self-help" book ever could have. It vitalized my understanding of what it means to be a child, a parent, and both at the same time. When I told Walt this, he kindly invited me to write this short foreword to his book.

Yet the book's value is not just in its many wonderful insights into parenthood (see "Introduction: You Are, You Are, You Are," "Joe's Nose," or "The Altar of Motherhood") or in its painful portraits of adolescence ("Commencement" and "County Fair") or in its rollicking humor ("Daughtertalk" or "P.U.T.T.T.") or in the author's warm and sometimes painful memories of childhood (see the entire first section). No, this book is important because on a deep level it isn't really about children and parents at all—in spite of its subtitle. It's about maturity—spiritual maturity—at all ages, a process that starts in childhood and should still be continuing when we enter, as the author says, that "city brighter than the sunlight."

Young people and old people, as Walter Wangerin describes, aren't all that much different from each other. We all battle sin and lethargy and selfishness and lack of love, and as a result, we're equally perpetual beginners in the tasks of growing, learning wisdom, finding maturity.

But that leads back to the original question. If we all need to grow, why does Jesus suggest that we become like children in particular?

Again, these essays suggest an answer. Jesus knew that children at their best can be more clear-sighted about spiritual things than adults (see the essay "Lookin' for Jesus in All the Wrong Places"). Childhood is the time for discerning moral choices, for plunging into the mysterious interaction of the outer world and the inner soul, for seeing life, if not always clearly, at least unobscured by the sophistications and sophistries of adulthood (read "My Shield and Portion Be"). As often as not, children see life in harsher and perhaps more eternal shades of black and white. I've seen far more children weep over wrongdoing than teenagers or adults—we who are so adept at justifying and rationalizing and finding good reasons for doing bad things.

It's a matter of sensitivity. What makes Walter Wangerin

such a wonderful guide to the life of the Spirit is that he is so articulate in describing our common lifelong struggle to be more aware of God, to open ourselves to His love and presence. If only we can be sensitive to Him—as children are—God, like the hero in an old play, is constantly bursting onto the scenes of our lives, flinging open the doors to let in the light, casting the villain into the wings, and miraculously remaking our world anew. In a sense, that drama is at the heart of every story in this book. Maturity, at whatever age it comes, is always a miracle. And this is a book about miracles.

Sensitivity has another face. While helping children discern truth, it also gives them a sense of wonder about the things that are. As I watch children discover the world—with all its vibrant newness and intrigue—I realize that I've lost much of that wonder. (See the essay "Turn and Become Like Little Children.") I grumble. I get harried and hurried. I take too much for granted, like spring days, motes in sunbeams, baby ducks, flying geese, lightning bugs, puffballs, shooting stars, jumpy frogs, funny-shaped clouds, ladybugs, and so on. I don't pause for them anymore. If told to look at a sunflower, for instance—to really look at it with the eyes of a child, the eyes of wonder—I'm afraid I'd get uneasy after about one minute. *So what am I looking for,* I would think. *What's the point?* Walt's essay "Spring Cleaning" is a reminder to me of wonder, for his mother's spring cleaning was not just work— in his child eyes, it was also a holy sacrament.

Sensitivity and wonder, finally, find their common ground in humility. After recommending childlikeness to his disciples, Jesus tells them, "Whoever humbles himself like this child is the greatest in the kingdom of heaven." Why are children humble? It may have something to do with what Jesus says shortly afterward, "I tell you that in heaven their angels always behold the face of my Father who is in heaven." A humbling thought. A mysterious thought. I can only wish—and pray— that I might change somehow so that my angel might do more of that beholding.

Increasingly, I'm fascinated by adults who seem childlike in the way that Jesus recommends. I wish I knew more of them. History and the arts abound with examples: St. Francis, for instance, and many of the saints of the church. In Japan, the eighteenth-century monk Ryokan and his contemporary, the haiku poet Issa (whom Robert Bly calls the world's greatest "frog poet"), were renowned for their love of children and for their own humility. In France, the poet Carmen De Gasztold (author of *Prayers from the Ark* and *The Creatures Choir*) and the early modernist composer Erik Satie (composer of the haunting "Gymnopedies") are remembered in much the same way. The British, of course, point with pride to hymn-writer and poet Christopher Smart (who wrote the sublime "Song of David" and the whimsically profound poem "I will consider my cat Geoffrey . . .") and the poet and visionary William Blake (whose poem "The Lamb" begins, "Little Lamb, who made thee?"—see the epigraph at the beginning of this book).

All these people were childlike, full of wonder, sensitive to spiritual things, which doesn't mean that they couldn't also be as complex and as difficult as children at times—a fact that should come as a relief to those of us who are often as childish as we are childlike. Another thing nearly all of these people had in common was that they were considered odd, even mad, by many of their contemporaries. Two of them, De Gasztold and Smart, even spent time in mental hospitals.

So now I'd like to ask a question: Who in modern America possesses this kind of childlike wisdom and wonder? Who among the famous is known for being courageously humble? Few celebrities, I'm afraid, and, sadly, few religious leaders. Even among American poets and artists, who would seem to be the most sensitive of all, the choice seems narrow.

One contemporary writer comes to mind, however, for he epitomizes the kind of child that Jesus loves to see in an adult: full of wonder, quick to sense the motions of God's Spirit, open to wonder and to humble convictions of sin. That man is the author of this book, Walter Wangerin, Jr.

To end this small foreword, I only need to add that my wife and I had a baby girl in June. Her name is Abigail. Now that she has finally arrived from that distant place, that other dimension, the only unimaginable thing about her is the pure joy she has given us. Now, nearly every night, as I rock her to sleep, I recite to her, "Little Lamb, who made thee? Dost thou know who made thee? . . ." by the childlike William Blake.

As she grows, I will pray that Abigail learns to be sensitive to truth, open to wonder, and alive to the love of God that surrounds her constantly. Part of that learning will take place as I share with her the stories in this and other books by Walter Wangerin and in the many stories and poems by writers like him who are not afraid to clamber onto Jesus' lap and sit there listening, wide-eyed, expectant.

Ultimately, it is not the little child nor the little lamb but you—the adult reader—to whom William Blake and Walter Wangerin address the question: Who made thee? Dost thou know? Dost thou *really* know?

Open yourself to Him. Become like a child and learn.

—Bob Hudson
Senior Editor
Zondervan Publishing House

Little Lamb,
Who Made Thee?

A Dedication: For my own four children—

T ell me, girl: how is it you can rust
A t three? The talk scrapes in your throat
L ike hinges like to bust;
I dle joints lock and loose on a corrosive note;
T iny flecks of oxide make your glances bold—
H ow is it, girl, that rust on you is just
A nother brown more beautiful than gold?

J ack Ketch, my sons have seen you!
O n a tight October morning have
S een you gibbet a million rattled leaves—
E ach leaf a sinew
P opped, each fall a potter's field and grave—
H ave seen you, Jack, and laughed at you!

M y sons heard rhythm in the falling leaves.
A rhythm's always an occasion for
T he dance, so they danced! They danced like the poor;
T hey thumped it like berries in a metal pot,
H arrowed together a mountain of compost gore,
E xcited the wind to a deeper declarative roar,
W ent down with a laugh they had not laughed before—

M ake three angels in the snow,
A geless, cold, and hollow;
R emind me once before you go
Y ou, too, were here—then follow.

You Are, You Are, You Are

*L*et the children laugh and be glad.

O my dear, they haven't long before the world assaults them. Allow them genuine laughter now. Laugh *with them,* till tears run down your faces—till a memory of pure delight and precious relationship is established within them, indestructible, personal, and forever.

Soon enough they'll meet faces unreasonably enraged. Soon enough they'll be accused of things they did not do. Soon enough they will suffer guilt at the hands of powerful people who can't accept their own guilt and who must dump it, therefore, on the weak. In that day the children must be strengthened by self-confidence so they can resist the criticism of fools. But self-confidence begins in the experience of childhood.

So give your children (your grandchildren, your nieces and nephews, the dear ones, children of your neighbors and your community)—give them golden days, their own pure days, in which they are so clearly and dearly beloved that they believe in love and in their own particular worth when love shall seem in short supply hereafter. Give them laughter.

Observe each child with individual attention to learn what triggers the guileless laugh in each. Is it a story? A game?

Certain family traditions? Excursions? Elaborate fantasies? Simple winks? What?

Do that thing.

Because the laughter that is so easy in childhood must echo its encouragement a long, long time. A lifetime.

But yesterday, even in my own community, these are the things I saw:

I saw a man walk toward me on the street, leading two children by the hand. His mouth was as straight as the slot of a mailbox, his eyes drawn tight as ticks. He wasn't looking at me. I greeted him. He did not answer. I greeted the children by name, the boy and the girl, and although these are our neighbors, I saw an instant and marvelous duplication: the children's mouths sucked in, as straight as mailbox slots; their eyes contracted, tiny and hard, like ticks. And I saw the cause of the change: the man, never yet glancing at me, had clamped their hands to silence.

Now, there may be many reasons why my neighbor would harden his heart against me. And some of these reasons may be reasonable. And perhaps it is not *un*reasonable that he should harden his children as well. But, while he has always carried his face like a cuttlefish, the boy had laughed quite blithely in my front yard the day before yesterday, and often the girl had made beautiful blushes of affectionate giggles when we spoke. They are changing. They are mimicking their elder.

And I saw a woman picking at her child, a baby no more than two years old. She was picking at him, pinching him, pushing him, prodding him forward as she walked and he trotted down the center of the mall. But the woman was scarcely aware of her own behavior. She was enjoying a conversation with another woman, friends out on a shopping trip.

But the baby couldn't maintain their adult pace. So she kept pushing his shoulders faster, faster—while his eyes grew huge with the fear of falling. Her eyes were fixed on her friend. Without looking at the kid, without ever losing the thread of her conversation, she interrupted herself to admonish him:

"Tad," she said—*poke, poke*—"keep moving."

"Go!" she snapped. *Poke!*

"Move it, dummy!" *Poke, poke, poke!*

Finally the woman stopped and, with her hand on her hip, actually looked at the kid. "Tad, what is the matter with you anyway?"

Well, he had sprawled face-forward on the ground. But he had gone down in perfect silence. Unto whom should he call for safety or support?

His mother was granting herself her own golden days—but at the expense of her son's. No one was laughing.

I saw a well-dressed man—a professional man, a man of success and genuine repute in our community—speaking in cool, indifferent tones to his daughter. His language was precise, articulate, intelligent, and devastating. No one could match his ironic contempt—least of all this adolescent. I think he thought he was being funny, that he was dealing with his daughter as an equal: two adults. Straight talk. No sentiment. No wishy-washy indirection. I think he thought his manner wonderfully restrained and civil; thus he could speak in public without embarrassment: "We communicate. We don't prevaricate. We tell the truth. We can take it." *Bang!*

But the truth he was imparting concerned her dress, her friends, her taste, and therefore herself. *Bang!* While his truth displayed his own self-confident intelligence and even his excellent, progressive method of parenting, it shot dead the child inside his daughter. An early death. Who was laughing then?

I heard inside a house two voices shouting. One belonged to an adult: "Brat! You never listen! I cook for you, I work for you, I bust my back and all I ask for in return is a little cooperation. Do I get it? No! What do I get from you? Nothing! Nothing! Oh, no, you don't! Don't you go rolling your eyes at me, baby brother—"

Two voices, but the one that belonged to the child was crying.

And I have heard the smack of human fury on human flesh.

And I have heard the laughter that children create on their own when their elders do not care. *That* laughter is bitter and sarcastic. That laughter declares with their parents: *Don't care. No, we don't care. No, nothing will get at us—*

And I've seen parents who, after seven years of not caring, suddenly rise up and fight on their child's behalf *against* the teachers, *against* some judgment of the educational or legal systems. These parents appear like heroes on the horizon, come to save their kids from systems which have, in fact, been trying to save the same children for the same seven years of parental neglect. This sudden, heroic passion on behalf of their kids is meant to prove parental love. It arrives too late. It looks too much like wrath to allow for laughter now. And these particular children ceased to laugh when they ceased to know their golden days—about seven years ago.

Sorrows such as these shall surely come—but surely, parents, not through us! Haven't we ourselves suffered the same abuses? Even as adults? And weren't they a misery more than *we* could stand? Isn't that motive enough to stop our tongues and stay our hands when we might wound our children? Do we need more?

Then hear this:

Children do not exist to please us. They are not *for* us at all. Rather, we exist for them—to protect them now and to prepare them for the future.

Who is given unto whom? Are children a gift to their elders? No—not till children are grown and their elders are older indeed. Then they are the gift of the fourth commandment, honoring hoary heads which have begun to feel past honor. But until then, it is we who are given, by God's parental mercy, to the children! And it is we who must give to the children—by lovely laughter, by laughter utterly free, and by the sheer joy from which such laughter springs—the lasting memory: *You are, you are, you are, my child, a marvelous work of God!*

Part I

The Child of His Parents

1

Spring Cleaning

*C*uriously, I've never thanked my mother for cleanliness. But I should. And I do.

Here comes the spring of the year. Here comes an air so laden and loamy, breezes so sweet I want to weep. Here come some of the purest colors of the earth: jonquils of unsullied yellow, the rouge of the redbud like the red breath of the forest itself, the white of the petaled dogwood like explosions of pillows. Here comes that scent after thunderstorm that is so like the warm, clean scent of wind-dried bedsheets against my cheek.

It stormed last night. For several hours there was a full cannonade of thunder and the heavy rain—and then the air had a dark, sparkling quality in my nostrils. Intoxicating. The night streets shined. All the earth was washed. Today the soil is shrugging toward rebirth.

And all this reminds me of my mother.

One particular gift of hers to us was cleanliness. The

27

experience of cleanliness, of becoming clean. We took it for granted; but it was a way of life, maternal virtue and holy consolation.

My mother kept cleaning, kept reclaiming territory by the act of cleaning it, kept redeeming her children therein.

And spring was always that fresh start of the faith and the hope in cleanliness, of the forgiveness of cleanliness, actually, since everything old and fusty *could* be eliminated, allowing the new to take its place—or better yet, the old itself could *be* the new again.

My, my, I haven't realized till now—sinking into a thoughtful old age—how dearly I loved spring cleaning.

Mom was happy, cleaning. She sang the winter away. She cracked old closures. Everything grievous and wrong and knotty and gritty and guilty was gone. Life returned, and sunlight and laughter and air.

She was a priest. This was her sacramental ritual. We children would wake in the early morning to a sudden bluster of wind through the house. Mom had thrown open all the windows upstairs and down, front and back, living room and our own bedrooms. The curtains blew in and clapped above us: *Get up! Get up! This is the Day of Atonement!*

We stumbled up to find that Mom had propped the front door open and the back door and the basement. We sailed through windy hallways.

Mother herself never paused the day long. She bound her hair in a bandanna blue with white polka dots; she wore weird pants called "pedal-pushers" and rubber gloves and a man's shirt and red canvas shoes with rubber soles: silent, swift, and terrible was she!

Rugs came up and were hung on lines outside for beatings. Her right arm got victories that day. Rugs coughed dark clouds into the yard, and then the hardwood floors were waxed with such power to such a marvelous shine that we, in sock-feet, slipped the surface, surfing. Clean is a feeling beneath your feet.

The curtains came down to be washed. The naked windows squeaked under Windex and newspaper. Mom's dust rag made the Venetian blinds clatter and complain. Bright light flooded the rooms. They seemed to inhale, these rooms, and so to enlarge themselves. Our house was growing. The furniture had to be moved back. In the huge, gleaming living room our voices echoed. Lo, we were new creatures, laughing with a louder sound and singing a sweeter treble than before.

Out with the old, then! Out with the bad. My mother was a purging white storm, focused and furious. Out with the sullen, germ-infested air, colds and flus and fevers. In with the spring! In with lily breezes!

In buckets Mom made elixirs of Spic and Span. She shook Old Dutch Cleanser on sinks as if it were a stick to scold. Throughout the house went ammonia smells, pine smells, soap smells, sudsy smells that canceled sweats and miasmas.

Winter clothes were washed and packed away. Summer wear appeared. Our very bodies lightened, brightened, beamed in newness and health.

I loved to be in my mother's house on such spring days.

Dresser drawers got new paper linings.

The closet hung straight and true.

By evening we ourselves were bathed, the dust of the day removed, leaving a creamy me.

And this, finally, was the finest comfort of the sacred day: that when I went to bed that night, I slipped my silver self between clean sheets. Sheets sun-dried and wind-softened and smoother to my tender flesh than four white petals of the dogwood tree. Delicious above me and below, blessing me and holding me at once: my mother's cleanliness. Such a sweet fastness of sheets declared the boy between them to be royalty for sure, chosen, holy, and beloved—the son of a wonderful queen.

Understand: the blessing embraced more than the house. The whole world seemed ordered and good in that day. My mother's feats of cleanliness persuaded me of universal kindness. I liked the world in which I dwelt, and I assumed it liked me, and I trusted it therefore.

Well, she sang when she cleaned. Her eyes flashed gladness. She had a plan, and she never doubted that she would accomplish it. Morning to night, I knew exactly where she was because her presence was a music, like birdsong, like the laughter of water.

What then? Why, then for me my mother *was* the springtime. She inaugurated it. She embodied it. She gave it her own peculiar and personal character. When she swept her right arm up, the firmament was made balmy and blue, and winter was over.

Never, never should children take so cosmic a gift for granted. "Cosmic," I say, because it defines our world for a while, and it teaches us whether to meet the real world hereafter with confidence and glad anticipation—or else with fears, anxieties, suspicions. We children inhabit twice the worlds our mothers make for us: first when that world is no wider than a house, a yard, a neighborhood, and then again when that world *is* the wide world—because her smaller world teaches us how to see and interpret the real world when we shall travel into it.

My mother made my infant world a clean, well-lighted place. Now, therefore, in spite of wretched evidence to the contrary, I continue to trust in the ultimate purity of God's universe.

My mother taught me the goodness of order and brightness. Now, therefore, I seek order in friendships and offer a bright unvarnished truth in return.

My mother assured me annually that newness has a right and a reality, that error can be forgiven, that the sinner can be reclaimed. In springtime she surrounded me with the immediate, primal light of God. Now, therefore, I trust renewal. Resurrection. Easter!

Surely, then, it is time to thank her.

With all my heart, Virginia, I thank you for the theology of your spring cleaning, the vernal sacrament. And how often, while we sat at worship in church, didn't you cock an eye at some smudge on my face? And how often didn't you spit on your handkerchief and with that most private cleanser, your personal scent, wipe the smudge away? Well, for that too, thank you.

I am washed within and without. I am myself the gift that you have given me, and all the world is the wrapping

Virginia Wangerin, Walter's mother

2

Lookin' for Jesus in All the Wrong Places

*E*arly in my childhood I suffered a spiritual crisis.

I can't remember now *how* early this was, but I was young enough to crawl beneath the church pews, small enough to be hauled back up by my mother one-handed, yet old enough to wish to see Jesus. I wanted to see Jesus with my own eyes. Ah, but I was also child enough to admit that I never truly had seen my Savior face to face. Never.

That was my crisis. Every Sunday everyone else who gathered for worship seemed so completely at ease that I was convinced they had seen God in his house. Everyone, that is, but me. They sang without distress. They prayed without regret. They nodded during sermons without a twitch of anguish, and I stared with envy into their peaceful faces. It was a party to which I alone had not been invited—in the Lord's own house, don't you see?

So who was it not inviting me?

I wanted desperately to see Christ Jesus strolling down

33

some aisle in a robe and a rope and sandals, eating a sandwich, maybe, since I would catch him off guard, just being himself. I spent all the time between Sunday School and worship peeking into every room, the pastor's study, the roaring boiler room, seeking the signs of his presence. Nothing.

Do you think he'd hide from me? Well, I knew he knew his house better than I did. He could hide. Do you think I made him mad by some sin I couldn't even remember now? I promise, I tried with all my might to remember. But I couldn't remember one *that* bad. As soon as I thought of it, I was right ready to confess and be forgiven. Until then I tried to surprise the Lord in hiding.

During services I would slip down from the pew to the floor and peer among ankle-bones and pants-cuffs and shoe-laces. So then, that's when my mother hauled me one-handed high onto the pew-seat again and clapped me to her side with a grip incontrovertible.

She's a very strong woman, my mother. You don't cross her. Once a forest ranger said, "If you meet a bear, you give the bear the right-of-way. Get out of there." Yeah, but my mother could silence whole congregations with a single, searing, righteous glance—so when she *did* meet that bear she beat two pans together until the bear backed down. "Woof," said the she-bear, astonished. "Not with *my* kids!" snapped my mother, uncowed. A very strong woman. Therefore I could not drop to the floor any more during worship.

But my yearning, imprisoned, increased to something like a panic.

I wanted to see Jesus!

The heart of a child is capable of great desolation and thereby of great cunning. The more I felt abandoned, the sharper became my baby wit, trying to figure where Jesus was hiding.

During one worship service, while the pastor stood facing a long wooden altar and chanting the liturgy, it dawned on me that the voice I heard was too rich to be his. This was a pale, thin preacher, but that chant charged the chancel like the King of Kings. Ha! Of course. The pastor was pretending. It was really *Jesus* who was chanting—Jesus, lying on his side in the altar-box, which was the size of a coffin, after all.

So, as soon as the final hymn was over and my mother's hard arm released me, I snuck forward, eyes ever on the altar to catch anyone else who might be sneaking away. Up the steps I went, right to the altar itself; and then I crept around to the side, and *YA-HA!*—I let out a loud shout to surprise the Lord in his tiny bedroom.

But nope. No Jesus. Nothing but dust and an old hymnal and a broken chair. And the angry arm of my mother, who hauled me home and caused me to sit on a bench for exactly the time of one more worship service.

The heart of a child can grow heavy with sorrow and loneliness. Why was Jesus avoiding me? Why did he take flight whenever I came near? Maybe it was my cowlick. I was not a pretty child. I knew that. Moon-faced, someone would say. Moony, generally. A daydreamer who frustrated folks who'd rather go faster. But—

But I really wanted to see Jesus.

Couldn't I see Jesus too?

Which room had I never checked? Was there any such room in the church? Was there somewhere all the rest of the saints made sure I didn't see?

Yes!

Oh, my, yes! Yes! My mother didn't know how helpful had been my time on the bench. It ended in pure inspiration. There was indeed one room into which I had never gone, nor ever so much as peeped—a sanctum of terrible mystery and terrible charm. It horrified me to think of actually entering the place. It tightened my loins and made me sweat all week long, every time I contemplated venturing that door. But I would. I wanted to see Jesus, and I was convinced that this room did above all rooms qualify for a Holy of Holies. Surely he was in that place where, if a boy came in unworthily, he would die on the spot.

And so it came to pass that on the following Sunday morning I wagered my entire life on chance that I knew where the Son of God lurked. That is to say, I risked my mother's wrath. During the sermon I flat slipped from the pew, ducked her reach, skipped down the aisle and tiptoed downstairs to The Dangerous Door, The Room of Sweet Folly and Holy Violence:

Breathlessly, I approached The Women's Bathroom.

The girls' *toilet,* you understand. Boys don't ever pass it without spasms of awe.

But I was determined. And the need had made me very bold. As bold as my mother.

I knocked. I nudged the door inward.

"Jesus? Are you in there, Jesus? Jesus?"

So then my life was over.

Nothing mattered any more. I was so hopeless when I returned to my mother in her pew that I felt no fear of punishment. She could do to me as she pleased, and it would mean absolutely nothing. Jesus wasn't in there. Mirrors and wide tables and weird smells were there; but the King of Creation did not dwell in the women's bathroom. Mom could kill me for all I cared. I had looked in the last place, and the last place was empty. There was no more.

Well, no, she didn't kill me. She froze me with a glance, blue-eyed and beautiful and severe: *Just wait, young man.* So what? She pointed to the front where the pastor in black was intoning: "This cup is the New Testament in my blood. . . ."

Blood. I guess she was indicating an ominous future for me. So what? What did I care?

"Do this in remembrance of me," said the gaunt, white, ghostly preacher, and then people began to move forward, pew by pew. They sang and they filed up the aisle.

My mother got up. She walked forward with them.

Surely I must have seen the ritual often before, but it

never had had so curdling an effect on me before. I was stunned by what my mother proceeded to do.

She acted docile! In a strange humility this strong woman knelt down before the pastor. She bowed her head. And then—like a child, like a *baby*—she raised her face and let him feed her! Yo! My mother can handle me. My mother can handle the neighbors. My mother can handle black bears in the Rockies—and my mother can surely handle herself. Yet now, as meek as an infant, she accepted a cracker from the preacher's hand. Then he gave her a little drink, and she didn't even touch the cup with her hands. She sipped at his bidding. My mighty mother, brought so low! What power could have stricken her so?

Yet, when she came floating back down the aisle and into our pew, there was nothing of defeat in her face. There was a softness, rather. Pliability and private smiling. She was different.

She smelled different, too. She came in a cloud of peculiar sweetness, a rich red odor. When she sat and bowed her head to pray, I stuck my nose near her nose, whence came this scent of urgent mystery. She felt my nearness and drew back.

"Mama," I whispered, "what's that?"

"What's what?" she asked.

"That smell. What do I smell?"

"What I drank," she said.

I wanted to pull her jaw down and look into her throat. "No, but what *is* it?" I begged. "What's inside of you?"

"Oh, Wally," she shrugged, reaching for a hymnal, "that's Jesus. It's Jesus inside of me."

Jesus?

My mother started to sing the hymn. I stared at her. Her profile, her narrow nose, her perfectly even brow all suffused with a scent of bloody sweetness. *So that's where Jesus has been all along. In my mama!*

Who would have guessed that this was the room in the house of the Lord where the Lord most chose to dwell? In my mama. Strong woman, meek woman, a puzzle for sure. My mama.

Well, I clapped my own small self smack to her side, and I took her arm and wrapped it around me to be the closer to them I loved, and we sang, and I grinned. I beamed like sunlight.

And I know we sang a heroic *Nunc Dimittis*: "For mine eyes have seen thy salvation. . . ."

. . . in blood, in a rich red smell, in the heart of my mama. Amen!

Wally, three years old

3

My Shield and Portion Be

*I*n those days homesickness seemed to curl in me like a little creature deep in my bowels. When it stirred, I suffered a sweet abdominal pain, like having to go to the bathroom. If it only stirred and stayed put, well, then I was okay. No one needed to know what was going on inside me. But if my homesickness grew worse and worse, that creature seemed to climb through my stomach into my chest. In the chest it was a suffocation, and I would puff and puff and suck air, and this would look like sobbing, but I wasn't sobbing, exactly. No, I was not crying. I was fighting the tears. I had not yet lost control.

But when the homesickness rose all the way into my throat, then it was a plain pain at the root of my tongue, and *then* I was crying. Then my sobs were huge gulps. And then almost nothing could console me, and everyone knew there was a problem with Wally.

I was often homesick, is how I understood the process so well.

But I had good reason to be.

I feared death. There was a lot of death around me.

Well—how does a kid know, when he has left behind him his home and his mother, his brothers and everything he loves, that they might not die while he is away? He wouldn't be there to save them in the event of disaster—and a kid just at the age of entering school can conceive of countless disasters.

Or who's to say the kid himself won't die away from home? And who would be there to hug him then, when his mother's absent?

Or, worst of all: what if his family just didn't care? What if they forgot the kid while he was gone? What if they finally decided that he was just too much trouble to put up with, so they all packed and moved away and he would find a shining empty house at his return? Well, whom would he go to *then* for help? The principal? Principals don't love small boys. He'd have to live on his own, forever sad that the thing he had feared actually happened exactly as he feared it.

Or what if he got lost on the way home? His mother would just cry her eyes out, so sorry, so sorry to lose her eldest, most precious son. So how could the boy live with himself, imagining the great grief he had caused his dear mother?

You see? All this is death. Different kinds of dying. But any one was a possibility.

That's why, on the first day of kindergarten, surrounded by strangers of various levels of confidence, the boy put his head down on the floor and cried. He feared death, and it made him unspeakably homesick.

That's why, when he was left with his Aunt Erna in St. Louis while his mother was in Chicago, he cried for two days together.

And again, the first day of first grade, he made it almost to lunch, but not all the way, and he put his head down on his desk, and the rest of the people looked at him. *Something's wrong with Wally.*

Yep. Something. The little creature of sorrow was clawing raw the back of his throat; his tummy felt completely empty, but his face was all full of sadness.

Death. He always lost, the kid did, when confronted with this lonely skull-bone of abandonment and death. But how could he defeat it? He was just a kid, a little one, weak, not strong. Not strong at all.

Yet that's exactly what my mother asked of me: "Oh, come on, Wally! Are you little or big?" she demanded, and I knew the answer she wanted, and I knew the truth. "Are you weak or strong?" she said.

I sighed and whispered, "Strong."

"Right!" she said. "Let's go."

Go our dusty ways to death, lonely, lonely on the way.

In the spring of my second-grade year, several months before the school term concluded, my whole family moved from Chicago, Illinois, to Grand Forks, North Dakota. My father had accepted a call to serve Immanuel Lutheran Church as its pastor. This church also maintained a parochial school, eight grades and kindergarten, though classes had to double up in rooms, one teacher taking several.

This meant that a little kid might meet some very old kids even in his classroom.

So, then, here we were in a completely new environment, a new neighborhood in which every face was strange, and even a new house, a huge house, a three-story house that made odd sounds in the night, keeping me awake with wondering.

So, then, I was completely unprepared for my mother's plans for me. *Surely,* I thought, *in the midst of so foreign a territory we need not increase the strain by dividing the family just now.* Surely she knew that the potentiality of death at separation had just shot up to plague levels.

They told me that tornadoes could come straight up from South Dakota and hit Grand Forks directly on the nose, just like that. They said, "Watch out!"

But my mother said, "I think you ought to go to school."

I said, "School's almost over for the year."

She said, "All the better to go now. Meet classmates now and they'll be your friends by next year."

I was aghast. Already now, even at this distant early stage, I felt the small creature stirring in the cradle of my loins. Sweet pain.

I said, "What about the tornadoes?"

She said, "What *about* tornadoes?"

"They'll probably come while I'm gone."

"Oh, Wally, that's utterly silly."

"I don't think so."

"Well, you don't know what's best. The sooner the better."

I said, "I don't feel very well."

She said, "Oh, come on, Wally! Are you little or big? What will your brothers think of you?"

So, then, in spite of the clear probability of death by disaster, my mother prevailed. She's a strong woman.

So, then: three of us drove on the following morning to the white wooden, two-story structure, Immanuel Lutheran School. Three of us. My mother, myself, and the creature deep within me, tickling the lower parts, stirring, stirring, threatening. Homesickness. But I said I wouldn't cry.

Mom took my hand and led me from the car into the building, up the stairs, and into a classroom. She introduced me to Miss Augustine, who was to be my teacher. This woman was beautiful beyond description, lithe and soft and tall, but she was a teacher. I hoped she would forgive me, but teachers by nature can be frightening, and even the smells were strange in this room, and the sunlight seemed cold and northerly and unkind. I felt a serious spasm of homesickness below my stomach. Therefore, as soon as Mom and Miss Augustine fell to talking together I slipped out of the room, down the stairs, out the door, and into the car, front seat. There I sat and waited for Mom to come back.

I persuaded myself that my mother would be delighted by

my decision, as relieved as I was to find that I would be going home with her after all today.

Well—no.

When she found me in the car, my mother opened the passenger door, put her hand on her hip, and demanded, "What's this? What's the matter with you? Wally, Wally, are you little or big? Are you weak or are you strong?"

I sighed and whispered, "Strong."

"Right! Let's go."

I huffed a little. I puffed a little. Things were swelling in my chest.

I sat in the back with the W's. Wangerin. A kid named Corky Zimbrick sat behind me.

I didn't talk. I didn't move. My face was already warm. My mother had driven away some time ago. I was alone. Danger zone. Homesickness had made itself felt in the regions of my chest. I *had* to hold completely still.

The beautiful Miss Augustine was saying something, teaching something to someone—but which class it was, mine or those older than me, I didn't know. All sound was like waterfall in my ears: a roaring.

Corky Zimbrick whispered in my ear, "Who are you? Are you the preacher's kid?"

Oh no, I was known! Someone actually knew me. It was like being snatched from hiding. I started puffing and puffing, sucking huge chestfuls of air. Homesickness was coming higher, almost too high to be controlled.

I raised my hand.

Miss Augustine saw it immediately. Extraordinary woman! Without a word she nodded full recognition of my request and permission thereto.

I got up and rushed out of the classroom, down the hall to the bathroom. I unzipped and stood up to the urinal, pretending to pee. All I wanted was to be alone for a while, to control the great grief rising within me—to stand perfectly still, to concentrate my energy on not crying. I said I was not going to cry this time.

Those were big urinals in those days. Big as a kid. Big as a closet. Intimidating. You stared straight forward at concave porcelain that seemed to be waiting for proof you belonged there.

Suddenly the door behind me banged open. With thunderous energy there entered an eighth-grade teenager, huge fellow. He recognized me.

"Hey, Wally," he shouted, bellying up to the urinal beside mine.

I recognized him, too, and I burned to be in his presence. This was Dicky Affeldt, the principal's oldest son. This was a man of the world, a wild and sinful sort. Just last Sunday I saw him in a deserted Sunday school room with an eighth-grade woman named Marcia. She had so many freckles all over her body that even her eyes were flecked with freckles. Well, Dicky Affeldt had her bent backward over a utility table and was kissing her on her freckled lips. And she laughed! She had actually laughed.

He said, "Hey, Wally," but I didn't answer him. I stepped closer to the urinal to hide that I was not peeing.

He started to whistle, making a torrent against the porcelain.

Then he looked at me. "What color's yours?" he asked.

I hoped he didn't mean what I thought he meant. This was becoming as frightening as I expected the world to be.

"What color's your pee?" said Dicky Affeldt. "Mine's clear," he said. "That happens when I drink lots of water."

Yep! Yep! He meant what I thought he meant. I was in the world, all right: treacherous, immoral, dirty, strange, and dangerous.

I zipped and raced out of there before I became the more involved. My mother should *know* what obscenities I had to deal with here.

Back in the classroom, back at my desk, I sat violently still, biting my teeth together as hard as I could. That little creature, homesickness and horror, had crept higher on account of the lewdness of Dicky Affeldt. It was nearly throat-high. It was almost uncontrollable. I breathed deeply, deeply, blowing air out at the nose, staring directly at the bottom left-hand star on the American flag—not crying. I said that I would not cry.

But then the worst thing happened, and I lost it.

They sang a hymn.

Hymns'll kill you.

All the kids in the classroom started to sing, "Blest be the tie that binds/Our hearts in Christian love—," and homesickness clogged my throat and squirted out my eyes. I burst into tears, sobbing, sobbing. I put my head down on the desk and tried at least to cry quietly. But I was crying, now. Nothing could stop it or console me. Nothing.

Miss Augustine called for recess. Kids began to rush outside.

"What's the matter with him? Isn't he coming?"

"Never mind," said Miss Augustine. "Never you mind, Corky Z."

So, then it was altogether still in the room. So I allowed some boo-hoos, some genuine shuddering sobs, all with my head down on my arms, down on the desktop.

Suddenly I heard humming beside me.

I peeped out underneath my arm and saw Miss Augustine sitting at the desk across the aisle from mine. She was huge in the little seat. She was grading papers. She glanced at me. Straightway I covered my face again.

"Walter Martin?" she said in soft voice. "Walter Martin, do you mind if I sit here?"

I shook my head.

"Oh, thank you," she said. "Sometimes I like to sit here when I do my work."

She began to hum again. Soon the humming turned into a little song, with words: *Jesus loves me, this I know—*

But then, in the middle of a line, she stopped. "Walter Martin?" she said. "Walter Martin, do you mind if I sing?"

I shook my head.

"Thank you," she said. "Sometimes I like to sing when I work."

—*for the Bible tells me so*—

Then she said, "Walter Martin, do you know this song?"

I nodded. I did. I had learned it last summer.

She said, "Well, then, do you want to sing it with me?"

Forever and ever I will recall with admiration that Miss Augustine was not offended when I shook my head, meaning no. It was in this moment that I began to love my teacher. Somebody else might have gotten mad because I wouldn't sing with her. But Miss Augustine, in her soft voice, said, "Oh, that's right. Little boys can't sing when they're crying, can they?"

She knew that she was not the problem, that I was.

She said, "Well, but do you think we could shout the song together?"

So then the children of Immanuel Lutheran School who were playing on the playground for recess heard two voices roaring through the windows, one fully as loud as the other:

"JESUS LOVES ME, THIS I KNOW! FOR THE BIBLE TELLS ME SO—" And I screamed as loud as I could, blowing the creature of homesickness out of my throat, dispelling sorrows and fears and mournings together:

LITTLE ONES TO HIM BELONG!
THEY ARE *WEAK*,
BUT *HE* IS STRONG.
YES!
JESUS LOVES ME. YES—

Yes, yes, yes. Jesus loves me. Yes.

Ah, Miss Augustine, teacher of natural skill and native insight into a kid's horrific fears: together we met death; we outfaced that specter together; and never have I forgotten the triumph. Once, while still I was young, death did not defeat me, but by a brazen shout and an expression of perfect faith, death itself—and homesickness too—was whipped. *Whupped!*

You shaped a boy, and forty years passed, and the boy became a man, and even today I declare the simple truth of *who* is strong after all, and who is weak, and in whose weakness power is made perfect.

Dear teacher, I heard recently that your smile is lopsided because a stroke destroyed the strength on one side of your face. Do you still shout your faith in the time of trial? The signs of dying? I do.

Last month my friend and my doctor, Stephen Ferguson, died suddenly and altogether too soon, leaving behind him two young children. No, three: his death reduced me to a child again. Homesickness stormed in me. I preached his funeral sermon—and I would have wept then except that first I had gone striding through a deep wood, roaring at the top of my lungs:

> JESUS LOVES ME, HE WHO DIED,
> HEAVEN'S GATES TO OPEN WIDE;
> HE WILL WASH AWAY MY SIN,
> LET HIS LITTLE CHILD COME IN.
>
> YES, JESUS LOVES ME!
> YES, JESUS LOVES ME.
> YES, JESUS LOVES ME—
> THE BIBLE TELLS ME SO.

4

’Twas Grace That Taught
My Heart to Fear

*I*n the summer of my seventh year I found an electrical cord in the kitchen and was immediately dazzled by its potential for wild, destructive power.

My mother was in the backyard mowing grass. She used a pushmower in those days, a clattering metal machine whose blades spun only when one drove the wheels forward with fierce energy. My mother possessed such energy. Brave, she was, strong enough to hit a softball farther than my father could, strong enough to punish a child with such rectitude he knew he'd met the forehead of the Deity. Whatever he'd done before she chastised him he would never do again. God had spoken in the arm of a mortal woman.

Clunk-whirrrr, went the mower outside. Thus I heard the power of her matriarchal arms: *Clunk-whirrrr! Whirrrr!*

Why I happened to be alone, I don't remember. I was the oldest of five and should have been baby-sitting. Dad was at church. Mom was busy. The children were my responsibility. Yet the kitchen was altogether mine, and I was alone.

And there was that black electrical cord. I drew it out of its drawer and pinched it as you pinch a serpent's neck, just behind the plug. The blinkless head. Two prongs like venomous fangs would strike and bite any socket in the wall.

The tail of the cord was a plume of naked copper wiring. The cord attached to nothing.

So, if I stuck this plug in a socket, there in the mild reddish metal would be such violent force that it could kill at a touch. *Yow!* Heaven and earth could collide at the command of a seven-year-old boy. My tummy tightened at the thought.

Well, and I knew the potency of electrical outlets. At the age of four I had managed to stick my right thumb into a living-room socket and had suffered a rapid, pulsing shock. It snapped my teeth shut and threw me backward across the room. My mother greased my poor thumb with butter, her healing of all horrors.

But here was a serpent that could suck juice from the wall and hold it in the bright ends of its tail—for *me! For* me rather than against me. This snake could strike with true authority where *I* willed it. I myself could hold a cobra of inestimable damage in my own two hands—

—if only I would, you know, plug it in—

Clunk-whirrrr! My mother labored in vigorous oblivion outside. I was alone. Nothing stopped me from arming my rattler. So I did. I thrust the teeth of this *Blitzschlange* into the socket by the refrigerator and stood back, pulling the cord out to length, staring at the copper scream of tail beneath my face—so close, so close to disaster! I began to grin. I could scarcely breathe because of my audacity.

But what good is the possession of power unless there's some evidence of it?

I began to wave my hand back and forth, swinging the snake's tail left and right, up and down in front of me. But nothing happened, of course. So I increased the speed, giggling, panting. Oh, I was scaring myself! Soon I was whirling the cord above my head like a lariat, barking a harsh, frightened laughter on account of such daring. I was so rash. Such a wild kid—

Suddenly, *crack-BOOM!* Copper wires struck the white refrigerator; yellow flame flashed forth; an explosion sent me backward, snatching the snake from its socket, and throwing me down on my butt against the far wall.

I held my breath a moment and surveyed the situation. I was alive. Not wounded. I had dribbled a little in my pants, but that dark shadow would pass. Here was the black cord dead across my legs. I—

Oh, no! Oh, *no!* Suddenly I saw that the refrigerator door had been scorched black by my sin. That yellow flash had burned white metal to a filthy char! Oh, no!

Clunk-whirrrrr! Mama, what are you going to do to me when you see this? *Clunk-whirrrrr! Whirrrrr!* I began to whimper. I dribbled a little more. Now I felt the fear I had not felt before, my mother being more deadly than a whole nest of serpents. My life was in jeopardy. Before nightfall I would be dead.

Clunk-whirrrr!

Well, then this wet child arose from the kitchen floor and minced toward the refrigerator and put forth his thumb and touched the black patch of his personal wickedness—and lo! Where he touched, he wiped it clean!

"Jesus, Jesus, thank you!" This child experienced a sudden honey-spurt of gratitude in all his muscles, so that he trembled and he lifted up his heart unto the Lord in joy. Black patches from electrical shocks can be erased after all! Sins and error can be canceled!

He ran for a rag and rubbed the mark away altogether, rubbed the white door white again, rubbed iniquity clean.

And so it was that at seven I did not die, neither from the bite of the serpent (which could have killed me, body and soul) nor from the wrath of my mother (which, far from desiring my death, desired my life, loving with an angry love, a dreadful love, a mother love alone).

I have since myself become an adult. And a father. A man who prays for his children with loud cries and tears, since his own experience has shown him how closely all children do creep toward the dangers. They could die! Even my beloved sons and daughters, unprotected by my love when I am outside and oblivious, could by their own hand die!

I pray: *O Lord God, save the children from danger, from the cunning of the Evil One, and from the disasters of their own stupidity!*

How often have they covered some sin to keep it from me?—my child, my children, in the fond notion that they could save their lives thereby, though it is the sin itself that can kill them!

Christ, let terror check them!

I love my children. Even in my sometime anger—especially then—I love them and beg your mercy upon them. Amen. Amen.

5

And Grace My Fears Relieved

*F*irst of all the love of God is a terrible thing. It begins by revealing unto us such treacheries and threats in the world that we know we must die soon—and until then (we are sure) we shall live in continual terror of the end to come.

The first act of divine love is to persuade us of the reality of death. We shudder and doubt that this can *be* love. We hate the messenger. We loathe such lovers. But it is a dear, necessary act nonetheless, because without it the second act of God's love would be altogether meaningless to us.

The second act is mercy. An absurdity of mercy. It is that God himself enters the same reality he first revealed unto us; he bows down and joins us under the same threat of death— and those whom he taught to fear he leads to safety. But those who do not fear do not follow. See? We had to suffer extremest fright in order to know our extreme need.

We who are under death must admit the peril; we have no other choice—except to die. Except to die.

But God, who exists above death, who knows no need at all, had the choice which we did not have. If, then, he emptied himself of power and humbled himself to death—even to death on a cross—this was purely an act of mercy on our behalf.

Then who can measure the love of God, to be thrice sacrificed: first, to be despised for declaring the terrible truth; second, to descend by choice into this treacherous and transient world; third, to save us by dying indeed the death he had revealed, dying it in our stead? Or whereto shall we liken so violent, valiant, and near an approach of the kingdom of heaven unto us?

Well—

The coming of the kingdom is like the coming of my father to my brothers and me when we sat fishing, blithely fishing, from a ledge twelve feet above the water in a stony cove in Glacier National Park.

In that year of sudden awakening, 1954, I was ten. My brothers, grinning idiots all (for that they followed a fool) were, in descending order, nine and seven and six.

Just before our trip west, I had furnished myself with fishing equipment. A Cheerios box top and my personal dime had purchased ten small hooks, three flies, leader, line, a red-and-white bobber, and three thin pieces of bamboo which fit snugly into one pole. Such a deal! Such a shrewd fellow I felt myself to be.

A leader of brothers indeed.

On a bright blue morning we chopped bits of bacon into a pouch, left the tent on high ground, and went forth fishing and to fish. We sought a mountain stream, though we ourselves did not depart the trail down from the campground. Fortunately, that same trail became a wooden bridge which crossed furious roaring waters, the crashing of a falls from the slower bed of a stream.

A mountain stream! There, to our right, before it dived

down into the rocky chasm below this bridge, was a mountain stream. Filled with fishes, certainly. We had found it.

But the bridge joined two high walls of stone, and even the slower stream came through a narrow defile.

But I was a shrewd fellow in those days, a leader, like I said. I noticed that a narrow ledge snaked away from the far end of the bridge, that it went beneath the belly of a huge boulder and therefore was hidden from the view of lesser scouts. If we could crawl that ledge on hands and knees through its narrowest part, ducking low for the boulder, why, we'd come to a widening, a hemisphere of stone big enough to sit on, from which to dangle our legs, a sort of fortress of stone since the wall went up from that ledge a flat twelve feet and down again from that ledge another twelve feet. Perfect. Safe from attacks. Good for fishing.

I led my blinking brothers thither. None questioned me. I was the oldest. Besides, I was the one with foresight enough to have purchased a fishing pole.

"You got to flatten out here," I called back, grunting in order to fit beneath the outcropping boulder. They did. One by one they arrived with me in a fine, round hideout. Above the sheer rock some trees leaned over and looked down upon us. Below our feet there turned a lucid pool of water, itself some twelve feet deep.

And so the Brothers Wangerin, Sons of Gladness and Glory, began to spend a fine day fishing.

We took turns with the pole.

The bacon didn't work, but—as a sign of our favor with all the world—the trees dropped down on silken threads some tiny green worms, exactly the size of our tiny hooks. We reached out and plucked worms from the air, baited the hooks, and caught (truly, truly) several fingerling fish. Oh, it was a good day! All that we needed we had.

Then came my father.

We didn't see him at first. We weren't thinking about him,

so filled with ourselves were we, our chatting and our various successes.

But I heard through the water's roar a cry.

Distant, distant: *Wally!*

I glanced up and to my right—where the water dropped over stone, where the bridge arched it—and I almost glanced away again, but a wild waving caught my eye.

WALLY! WALLY! WALLY!

"Dad?" Yes!—it was Dad. "Hey, look, you guys. There's Dad leaning over the bridge."

They all looked, and straightway Philip started to cry, and then Mike, too. Paul dropped my pole into the water twelve feet below. And I saw in our father's eyes a terror I had never seen before.

WALLY, HOW DID YOU GET OVER THERE?

Over here? I looked around.

Suddenly *here* was no fortress at all. It was a precipice, a sheer stone drop to a drowning water, and *that* water rushed toward a thundering falls far, far below my father. With his eyes I saw what I had not seen before. In his seeing (which loved us terribly) I saw our peril.

He was crying out as loud as he could: *WALLY, COME HERE! COME HERE!*

But the ledge by which we'd come had shrunk. It was thin as a lip now. The hairs on my neck had started to tingle, and my butt grew roots. I couldn't move. Neither did my brothers. I didn't even shake my head. I was afraid that any motion at all would pitch me headlong into the pool below. I gaped at my father, speechless.

He stopped waving. He lowered his arms and stopped shouting. He stood for an eternal moment looking at us from the bridge, and then his mouth formed the word, *Wait*. We couldn't hear it. He didn't lift his voice. Quietly under the booming waters he whispered, *Wait*.

Then he bent down and removed his shoes. At the near end of the bridge, he bent down farther, farther, until he was on his stomach, worming forward, knocking dust and pebbles

AND GRACE MY FEARS RELIEVED

by his body into the stream, bowing beneath the enormous
boulder that blocked our freedom.

"Dad's coming. See him?"

"Yep, Dad's coming."

"I knew he would."

He pulled himself ahead on the points of his elbows, like
the infantry beneath barbed wire, his face drawn and anxious.
He was wearing shorts and a long-sleeved flannel shirt. Red
with darker red squares. I remember.

When he came into our tiny cove, he turned on his belly
and hissed to the youngest of us, "Mike, take my heel." Mike
was six. He didn't.

"Mike, *now!*" Dad shouted above the waterfall with real
anger. "Grab my heel in your hand and follow me."

You should know that my father is by nature and
breeding a formal man. I don't recall that he often appeared in
public wearing short-sleeved shirts. Nor would he permit
people to call him by his first name, asking rather that they
address him according to his position, his title and degree.
Even today the most familiar name he will respond to is
"Doc." Dad is two-legged and upright. Dad is organized,
controlled, clean, precise, dignified, decorous, civil—and
formal.

What a descent it was, therefore, and what a sweet
humiliation, that he should on his stomach scrabble this way
and that, coming on stone then going again, pulling after him
one son after the other: Michael, Philip, Paul.

And then me.

"Wally, grab my heel. Follow me."

It wasn't he who had put us in these straights. Nevertheless, he chose to enter them with us, in order to take us out
with him. It was foolishness that put us here. It was love that
brought him.

So he measured the motion of his long leg by the length
of my small arm, and he never pulled farther than I could
reach. The waters roared and were troubled; the granite shook
with the swelling thereof. But my father was present, and very

present. I felt the flesh of his heel in my hand, leading me; and I was still in my soul. I ceased to be afraid.

That stony cove had not been a refuge at all but a danger. Rather, my father in love bore refuge unto me; my father bore me back to safety again. So I did not die in the day of my great stupidity. I lived.

Thus is the kingdom of heaven likened unto a certain man whose eldest son was a nincompoop—

6

But When I Became a Man

I remember the difficult ritual of my confirmation—when at the age of thirteen I stood in front of the whole church and confirmed my faith in my Lord Jesus.

It felt that it happened wrong for me.

In fact, it happened right; but that feeling of personal terror was a measure of the personal, important, and public step this infant took toward adulthood. Spiritual and communal independence is, when it is real, a scary thing.

My confirmation class consisted of five students. There were two girls, sisters, who commonly pulled my hair on Saturday mornings, protesting in thick accents that they liked me, they *liked* me, then falling absolutely silent when the pastor arrived and the lesson began. They were Dutch immigrants, strong as to muscles, weak as to English. There was one boy who truly did befriend me but who could memorize nothing and who likewise subsided into an unteachable silence when actual class work began. There was a boy who set himself in direct, perpetual competition with me, a glittery-eyed bird of a fellow, a crouching raptor-bird of a fellow. And then there was me—bespectacled, small of stature, grotesque as to hair in which I suffered explosions of cowlick on the back of my head, and as to intellect, passable. I could memorize. Well, and I *had* to memorize, didn't I? In those days my father was the president of Concordia College in Edmonton, Alberta, Canada, a Lutheran, Christian institution. His reputation, therefore, would be affected by my public performance of matters faithful and pious—and that's exactly what was coming: confirmation started with an examination in front of the whole congregation and all my family and God and everybody. Dad is "Walter." I am "Walter." I am his oldest child. I had to uphold the name. I memorized. I memorized everything in the catechism. I memorized *both* the answers *and* the questions *and* the Bible passages that proved those answers to be right.

I ate that book like Ezekiel.

Grim.

I had to.

So on Saturday mornings Pastor Walter Schoepf said to one boy, "What does this mean?" And that boy always said, "Umm. Umm." He didn't know.

So the pastor turned to the two sisters and said, "What does this mean?" Well, but they remained serenely innocent of questions and answers and reputations and English, too. No fears of failure in them. No pressures on their pretty heads.

So then the pastor—all he had to do was say, "Wally." He didn't even have to say again, "What does this mean?" because I memorized questions. Just looked at me and said, "Wally"— and I popped up and recited: "I believe that Jesus Christ, true God, begotten of the Father from—"

All at once (but so regularly that I grew gun-shy in my recitations, waiting for this attack) the competitive fellow, unable to contain himself longer, erupted knowledge, trembling and shouting: "ALSO-TRUE-MAN-BORN-OF-THE-VIRGIN-MARY-IS-MY...."

There was much to wrack my nerves.

So much depends, so much depends, so much depends upon Wally....

The day of confirmation drew near. One week away.

My mother took me downtown to shop. We got me new underwear, new shoes, a shirt, and a new blue suit. Expensive raiment. All this made my heart pound, thinking, thinking: *They're putting money into this thing!* They loved me, of course. They expected me to do well—and to be worthy of a new blue suit.

Would they, then, in the actual event, be proud of me?

On Saturday—our last class, the day before The Day— the Dutch sisters pulled my hair. Routine. But it hurt. And it made me think about my looks for tomorrow. I decided that they pulled my hair because the cowlick invited exactly such scorn. The cowlick, as it were, deserved it.

So that night I took a careful bath, cleaning everything with a scrubbing brush. Toenails. Ears. My whole unbeautiful body. My mortified face. It's too bad I didn't have good looks. But maybe I didn't deserve good looks. *That raptor-bird boy had a certain glittering intensity and dark grooming that made him good-looking.* I thought of my competition, and I thought: *Well, but there is one thing I can do,* and I did—

When I got out of the tub, I didn't dry my hair. I combed it dripping wet. Then I got a nylon stocking from my mother's drawer and rolled it up into a tight hat and put it on my wet, straight hair and rolled it down again over my ears. I wore it to bed. I planned to have perfect hair tomorrow. That's what I could do for my mother and her expectations and her expensive blue suit, for my father and his reputation and our name. At least I could have one perfect thing.

So much depends upon a Wally beautiful with learning—

I lay perfectly still. I prayed a lot that night. Mostly the

Lord's Prayer, though, because I kept losing my place in the middle and had to start over and over again. Pastor Schoepf kept coming in and saying, *What does this mean?* Somebody would quote part of the Apostles' Creed, "—And in Jesus Christ, his only Son, our Lord," and then Pastor Schoepf would interrupt and say, *What does this mean?* So I kept losing my place in the Lord's Prayer—which I wasn't saying from memory so much as really trying to pray it.

Well, at that time I was already the oldest of seven sisters and brothers. My confirmation was the first. And Aunt Erna had come all the way from St. Louis because she was my sponsor at my baptism, and she told me that she had a present for me, and she even told me what it was: a King James Bible with onion-skin pages, a very delicate thing; but she also said that she wouldn't give it to me until after my examination, so I better do well in this examination.

So much depends upon ...

On the morning of the Sunday of my confirmation I put on my new underwear and my new shirt and my new blue suit. I went into the bathroom. Standing in front of the mirror I rolled up the nylon stocking, careful not to muss a hair on my head. The front looked flat, wispy, obedient, very nice—

But suddenly there shot up from the back of my scalp a whole rooster tail of a cowlick! Oh, no! Oh, *no!* It was like a broom sticking up. It was huge and waving and happy to be there, like it wanted to come to the party, too. I pressed it down with the flat of my hand, and that actually hurt the roots. It just jumped up again. *Oh, no, dear Jesus, no! No!* What would people say about me now?

I took a brush. I flooded it with water. I slicked and slicked my hair until the cowlick grew too heavy to rise again. I was, with great perturbation, drowning a cowlick, killing it. I wanted it dead on the Sunday of my confirmation.

So, then, my father drove me to church, his grim and

dripping Ezekiel. I got to sit in front. Mom sat in the back seat. They let me out first.

So, then, I was walking up the path to the church door, my back to the car, wondering whether they were watching me and whether they were proud of me now, whether maybe they were even mentioning out loud to one another that this was their oldest son about engage in an act of extraordinary courage—when I felt one single cowlick hair pop up: *Ping!* Immediately I reached back and yanked it out and kept on walking.

So, then, all five of us dressed in white robes behind the pastor—the confirmation class—processed up the aisle of the sanctuary while the congregation stood on either side singing a hymn. The church was absolutely jammed with people. I kept my eyes properly forward, but I couldn't sing. There was no spit left in my mouth. I was the shortest confirmand—so how was I to maintain dignity and uphold the family name? A hair popped up. With one hand I covered my mouth to cough; but the cough was a fake to hide what my other hand did; it plucked that hair out of my head.

Finally we sat down upon five chairs that were arranged like a little U in the chancel, our backs to the congregation (but we could hear and we could feel the overwhelming weight of so many people leaning forward to listen and to judge). Pastor Schoepf stood up in front of us rubbing his hands. About to begin. He had the questions on a sheet of paper. We were supposed to have the answers in our heads. A hair popped up on the back of mine and began to wave to the congregation. This time I didn't try to hide the gesture: I pulled it out.

Today as an adult, a father and a pastor too, I declare that my terror in that moment—caught, as it were, between the millstones of responsibility and fear—had its holy purpose. Our present society has few true rites of initiation by which a child can leave childhood and enter, through the valiant accomplishment of a significant task, adulthood with all its rights and responsibilities.

How is he to know that a change has taken place, both in him and in the community's regard for him? How is her very soul to recognize that she must—and can!—shoulder a new role? And how is the community itself to be persuaded to treat the individual differently hereafter? Such a radical shift both in self-awareness and in communal relationships requires an event to mark the change and actually to effect it. It doesn't always happen by unconscious development. In fact, precisely because we *don't* attend as well to such rites of initiation as cultures foreign, primitive, and past, we are a society infested with grown-ups stalled in their childhood, people of age still stuck in immaturity, people unable or unwilling to take responsibility for themselves, people as self-absorbed as children because they are, in spirit if not in body, children.

Their chrysalis never broke nor opened. They never emerged completely whole and capable of high, frightening, independent flight. There never was a rite.

But such ritual must be, as all rituals are, an *event.* And that event must involve a *task* to be accomplished by the initiate. The task, then, must be a personal *experience,* not merely some received piece of information or money or status without the fear and the possible failure of personal action. It must be an experience which relies on the self and God alone, so that the initiate can truly feel the new definitions of her being and the change they represent. Such persuasion comes not so much by words and teaching as by crisis and survival. The task must be *significant,* not some safe parody of adult duties, not a "cute" conferring of honor upon children for no deserving except that we love them. If it is significant—crucial to one's future, so difficult as to threaten failure and, at the same time, to honor success with an honest praise—then passing the test is a genuine entrance into adulthood. Finally, the task must be *public.* The whole society might then honor and admit the change of one individual, receiving noisily a new adult within itself as a responsible citizen.

Confirmation was my initiation.

I can conceive of nothing more significant than that I should, of my own heart and strength and mind, confirm that God is God and is my Lord. This was not some childish entertainment for my congregation. This was in fact a matter of life and death. I knew so by the great burden placed upon me, father and mother and aunt and people. I know it better now for the greater consequence of faith. Life and death: this was no cliché. I would live or die by this divine relationship. Lo, I was crossing into a maturity of faith. In baptism Jesus claimed me. Confirmation, now, completed that holy moment as I independently and with full knowledge claimed him: my Lord.

Terrible, terrible, beautiful! Filled with anxiety before the task, because of the task, because of its monumental importance; trembling, swallowing, standing here at the edge of adulthood, standing here on the precipice 'twixt heaven and hell—

Pastor Schoepf glared at the Dutch girls with a sort of haggard fear. He had already endured three *Umm*s and silence from the poor boy who could memorize nothing. The pastor now said to one sister, "What does this mean?"

"*Vass?*" she said, blinking.

He turned to the other sister, "And in Jesus Christ, his only Son, our Lord. It's the second article of the Creed. What does this mean?"

The second sister smiled blithely, showing two stalactites of teeth, monsters of white indifference. The pastor swallowed, glanced at the heavy ocean of folks behind us, and said, "Wally, please, what does this mean?"

I stood up.

That small motion caused a bush of hair to spring up from the back of my head, nodding and grinning at the congregation. I was tempted to tear it out in tufts and handfuls, furious that the one thing which I had hoped would be perfect turned out to betray me. That laughing cowlick! That uninvited idiot! That ugliness—

In the minute while I stood hesitating and Pastor Schoepf's expression grew more and more desperate, my competitive classmate started to answer in a low hiss: "I-believe-that-Jesus-Christ-true—"

And a marvelous thing occurred.

I thought, *I can do this myself,* and straightway, at the top of my lungs, I began to bellow: "NO, NOT YOU, GERALD—*I* BELIEVE THAT JESUS CHRIST, TRUE GOD—"

Such a rush of holy energy blew through me that I *loved* the thing I was saying. I was not reciting. I *meant* it. I meant it with so complete a joy that I forgot about my cowlick.

"—JESUS CHRIST, TRUE GOD, BEGOTTEN OF THE FATHER FROM ETERNITY—"

Oh, I boomed the affirmation. I shouted sweetly oblivious of anyone else's opinion or judgment. I had broken *through!*

"—AND ALSO TRUE MAN, BORN OF THE VIRGIN MARY—"

While I roared forth the words of my own stout heart, I truly forgot about my father and his reputation, my aunt and her gift, the pastor and my classmates and anyone else whom I was supposed to represent except God, except my God. Was my mother proud of me?

O let her be proud forever of this (for by this I rose on my own strong legs and took my stance among the saints), that I turned to the church and shouted with baby abandon:

"THAT JESUS IS MY LORD!"

7

How Precious Did That Grace Appear

Now, then, *Grace.*

Ever since I was a tiny child, I knew that word. In confirmation class I had memorized its meaning as an attribute of God: "Showing undeserved kindness, forgiving." More than a characteristic of God, I learned that it is also an *act* of God. But in those days I received this stuff neat, in a doctrine which was itself not an act but a definition: "God loves me when I am unworthy of love. He grants me salvation which I could not purchase. Forgiveness is a free gift of Jesus, and grace transforms the sinner since God's love makes the unlovely lovely indeed."

"What is grace?" Pastor Schoepf had asked during the confirmation examination.

And I had answered by quoting the passage from Ephesians 2:8–9: "For by grace are ye saved through faith; and that not of yourselves: it is the gift of God: Not of works, lest any man should boast."

I was a smart kid.

And yet I did not really know what I was talking about. *I* had just accomplished this most difficult task. I did it. Therefore, although I could speak well and wisely of grace, that was in itself the problem which condemned me: I *could* speak of grace, even glibly and casually. I was not struck dumb by the impossible beauty of the thing. I was not overwhelmed by the absolute absurdity, the flat illogic, the utter conundrum of this act of God.

Grace should not be.

In fact, by every moral and human right, grace *cannot* be.

Nevertheless, it is.

And without it, we die.

One ought to lay one's hand upon one's mouth in the presence of such a thaumaturge and answer nothing. One ought to confess that he has spoken without knowledge, that he has uttered things too wonderful for him, and so repent in dust and ashes.

But I was self-important in those days. I had not actually experienced love when I knew I didn't deserve it.

Doctrine may teach us the definitions of our faith's most fundamental truths; but the truths themselves elude us until we meet them ourselves and *experience* them: meet them, greet them, and find ourselves to be borne aloft by them. Then we know what hitherto we'd only learned by rote.

Grace: this is how I, I myself, first encountered it.

The Canadian winter of 1957 was very hard. Life in general was growing harder and harder by the month, but I felt it right that I should shoulder my load in life, since I had that previous spring been confirmed and had entered adulthood thereby. Oh, yes, I took my new station very seriously.

To me adulthood meant you did your duty yourself, without complaint. Certain honors were accorded the adult; but certain obligations were required in return. The honors sounded like this: "You're free, young man." I myself could, for example, choose what time I went to bed. But the obligations sounded like this: "Young man, you're on your own."

I was alone.

Therefore, I bore my responsibility within the family. I was the oldest of seven by then. I saw to the welfare of my sisters and brothers. I made sure they went to bed. I hollered at them.

My mother said, "Who died and left you boss?"

I said, "Yeah, but—" like any debating adult. "Yeah, but they ought to be quiet. Yeah, but they need their sleep. Yeah, but I'm only doing what *you* do, Mom."

My mother was in trouble in those days. I was helping her.

But she said, "Why aren't you in bed?"

I said, "I'm grown now."

"Grown," she said. "My son is grown." She folded her arms and stood back to get a better look. "And can he reap the whirlwind too," she said, "this man of mine?"

My enigmatic mama. Well, but I knew what she meant: *You're on your own, boy.*

Yes. No argument. I was so much on my own that even my mother didn't know that I had chosen to help her, nor could she know the cost. I was protecting her. She and my father had begun to suffer the malice of certain bitter people. A scourge of gossip swept our city, truly wounding my parents since this nastiness was directed at them in particular. Well, and I had seen the hurt in their faces. Slashed by loud lies. Their solid work riddled by whispers. Gossip is a sort of guerrilla warfare: it hits and quickly disappears before there can be a genuine engagement. Liars hide. And my mother sometimes sobbed in secret. But I heard her. I knew. Therefore I had taken it upon myself to keep at least their household peaceful. Yes, I bossed the kids to goodness, to silence, and to bed, and then I withdrew myself to consider the trouble my parents endured.

Winter was very hard that year. I felt lonely in my

adulthood. But I accepted that loneliness uncomplainingly, as the due of an adult.

So be it. I would live with it. Forever.

And then one night I couldn't sleep at all. I was sick. My stomach kept knotting in spasms, and by two in the morning I had dampened the sheets with sweat. There was a winter wind outside, whistling at the eaves with the sort of solitary note which made my corner of the bedroom dark and lonely indeed. Awake this way, I seemed to be alone in the universe.

Now, I expected absolutely nothing. It never occurred to me but that I would have to handle this misery alone. I was an adult. Free. On my own.

But I must have been groaning out loud.

Because suddenly the hall light came on outside my door. Then the door swung inward. And there stood my mother, dark in a diaphanous white gown. Calm, quiet, and utterly beautiful.

"Wally, what's the matter?"

I was stunned. This I had not expected. Her presence and her voice alone—the familiarity of a voice which I had thought I'd never hear that way again—made me start to cry.

But I was fourteen years old then.

"Wally?" she whispered.

"My stomach," I sobbed.

"Oh, Wally!"

My mother floated toward me then and sat on the edge of the mattress, which sank to her weight. She put a cool hand to my forehead. "Yes, fever," she said. How long since she had sat beside me so? How long since she had kissed the little Wally? Long.

In the dark, her hair a nimbus by the hall light, she whispered, "Pull your knees up to your tummy. It'll ease you."

How holy the homely remedies! I did, and I cried and cried—for none of this should have been. I truly never thought that I could be a child again. Oh, I thought I had lost all that.

But I had a mother, after all, and she came to me. I was exhausting myself by protecting *her* in those days, not she me—and yet she came to me. I was fully adult, independent, self-sufficient, a reaper of the whirlwind, accepter of all the consequences; I had forfeited the tender mercy of a mama in the nighttime. Nevertheless, she came to comfort me—and like a baby I curled into the crook of her arm and wept.

Grace: It is the clear and uncontested *not* deserving which makes the gift so sweet and potent.

Grace: This was the first most memorable time that grace embraced me. A thing I felt, a truth I experienced, a mother who came in spite of the probabilities.

Grace: In the countenance of my sudden mother was the love of my healing God, all unexpected but manifestly here. And behold: my tummy stopped hurting. Was it the knees drawn up? Was it some charm of the woman who touched my forehead? No matter. My mother's son in that moment was healthy and lovely and lovely indeed.

Part II

The Pastor of Children and Parents Together

8

Turn and Become Like Little Children

G ive us, O Lord, clean eyes, uncomplicated hearts, and guileless tongues.

Make us like children again!

Here is an irony: when we are still children, we might be the best that we're ever to be—yet we yearn to throw off childhood. We rush to teenagerhood, a worser state in every way, all the while thinking we're getting better.

Let me explain. . . .

When we are children we're likelier to be kinder because we are small in an overwhelming world, and smallness keeps us humble. We identify with them the world considers inferior, helping the helpless and the infirm.

But children wish they weren't children. Smallness is itself a bafflement, a vulnerability. Children rush, therefore, toward the biggerness and the blunt authority of their betters, the teenagers.

Again. . . .

When we are little children we're likelier to be honest. That doesn't mean we're likelier to be *right*; but the honesty alone—our inability to say anything except what we ourselves see of the world—is wondrously effective and refreshing. "But the king has no clothes on!" cries the kid, an observation both honest and right and therefore revolutionary in a kingdom where politics means sucking up and where favors are earned by flattery.

Ah, but that same kid wishes he were older. Soon enough, then, he learns to dissemble, and soon he is buttering his peers, if not his elders—and then he's a teenager surely.

And again. . . .

When we are wide-eyed children the world is filled with things both visible and invisible, things material and immaterial. We make no distinction between the two. There are ghosts. There is also God. These are as real as the walls of our bedrooms and the mouths of our mothers. And that which is real we honor by obeying, by accommodating its presence in our lives and our behaviors. We fear the ghosts. We pray to God.

And we ourselves are spiritual beings too, therefore: small bright bundles of body-and-soul. There is a glory around our heads of which we're unaware but which renders us radiantly lovely since those who see angels do shine as well an ethereal light.

But children are soon ashamed to be children. They're dazzled, rather, by the cold (and self-protective) cynicism of punk teenagers for whom nothing is honorable, by whom nothing need be obeyed (or else one loses one's rep, one's rap, and one's glory). The world of the teen seeks matter and sensation, sound and color and clothes and spasmodic satisfactions—and everything spiritual proves to have been a conspiracy of elders to keep their children on chains.

So we rush to throw off the best we might ever be and to

put on instead the dead-slouch, know-it-all, hard-as-steel, lank-lipped sneer of the cynic.

So we are children no longer. This wish is always granted slower than we would and sooner that it should—but this wish is always granted.

Yet, when we were children we laughed without embarrassment. We hooted and giggled and roared till our sides cracked and our cheek muscles ached. The unself-conscious laughter rang very true, like bells in a blue sky, and therefore taught our elders themselves how to laugh again.

When we were children we could gasp with delight at a sudden, beautiful thing, yearning to touch it. We didn't worry whether our notions of beauty were naïve. We didn't pretend sophistication. We were not proud; therefore, we could not be humiliated. But our unsullied joy was itself like leadership to all God's creatures, a call to be at peace together.

When we were children our loving was given immediate expression. We *said* it. We *showed* it. We would throw our arms around beloved people and kiss them and purr to be kissed in return. No one had to guess whether we loved. Nor did love seem either a weakness that must be hidden or else a physical desire that must be gratified. Love made us happy. We liked to be happy. And so we were leaders even of whole countries into the image and the command of God—Who *is* Love.

When we were children we accepted forgiveness completely. It truly did—when it was truly given—ease us and allow us to begin again, *anōthen,* as new as one just come down from heaven. We could bounce back from the most grievous sins so quickly that adults wondered whether we had truly repented. Oh, we had repented. Children can move to sorrow instantly and instantly to gladness again, yet feel both moods profoundly. This is the emotional nimbleness of those who have not yet sickened their feelings with self-analysis nor thickened their motives with ambition.

Those who fly swiftly to delight, who fear not to express their love, who believe completely in forgiveness—well, they are fearless. And so it is that the sucking child plays blithely on the hole of the asp, and the weaned one scares her elders by putting her hands on the adder's den.

But then—children don't want to be children.

They want to grow hair in smooth places, immediately to cut it off again.

They want to smear outrageous colors on places God had painted pink and to punch holes in places God had made smooth. This is called "style."

They pretend to love the things they don't and feign indifference for things they love unspeakably. This is called "fashion."

Because their peers do, they walk in streets instead of on sidewalks; they wear jeans beaten old before the purchase; they do not lace their tennis shoes; they congregate on corners like lemmings going nowhere, doing nothing. This is called "doing my own thing."

They laugh when it isn't funny and do not laugh when it is. This is called "cool."

When they don't feel something, they act as if they do, and they exaggerate the act for fear that someone may notice it's only an act. They fear to be different from peers. When, however, they feel an emotion deeply (whether rejoicing or love or repentance) they mask the mood and gaze wanly into the distance.

They are not what they are; and what they are they strive to hide. This is called "teenager." It is considered an advance over childhood. It's the rush from innocence into society. It's a determined dispersal of the clouds of glory which we trailed when first we came from God.

It is a pity.

"Give us clean eyes, uncomplicated hearts, and guileless tongues, O Lord!"

That, immediately, was my prayer when I found among my letters the following, unself-conscious "summery" by Erica Ulrey. Her grandmother had read to the child a book of mine. The book was about Jesus. Then Erica took pen and printed on paper and mailed to me these words:

SUMMERY JESUS STORY

Well it all started out when an angle came to mary and told her that she was going to have a baby, it would be a boy, a boy name jesu. He would be the son of the Lord. They traveled to drusilem. They knocked on inkerp's door but know one had room. So they went to a stable. She had the baby. Jesus grew older when he was 20 or 30. He went and told stories. He got bapties because he wanted to have sins. He told Peater that his enimes would kill him. Jesus arived in drusilem on a donkey. Children were waving palm limes. Jesus went in two the Temple and open the cages of animals tiping taples. His enimes came and hung him up on a cross. After three day's his desiples came to his grave, and angle stood in front of his grave. He was not in the grave. They found Jesus. They thought he was a gost but he had the holes in his hands. Then one day Jesus said I will be up in hevan. The End.

O sisters and brothers (so often so teenish in spite of our years, because we desire the approval of peers) if we would turn and become like little Erica, then such fearless and faithful contemplations of the gravest mysteries need never end for us as well.

No, not ever: for it is as little children that we shall enter the kingdom of heaven.

9

I Love Thee, Baby B

*B*randon Michael Piper. What a sober name for a two-year-old! It sounds senatorial. It seems an executive's name.

But you bear the big name well, my little godson. You've a stalwart constitution and a sweetness of spirit that softens me when I hold you. No, the name is not too large; rather, you make the name foursquare and strong.

Dear Brandon:

Perhaps you won't remember in the years to come (but I will always remember) that I am the one who holds you these Sunday mornings during Bible class. Your mother and your father both have duties; but I have two arms free and a large heart, and I am your godfather, and I love you.

You cling to me, child. Stump-arms soft on pliable bone, you grip my neck. You lock your legs around my body. I couch your butt on my forearm and press you to my chest and feel the deep warmth of your trusting infancy. Oh, Brandon! You hallow me with such trust! You make me noble and kind.

They call you "B," don't they? "Baby B." A lighter, lesser name than the one you'll carry into adulthood but one conferred by affections. I remember when I was trying to distract you in Bible class and happened to draw that letter. You read it. You astonished me by the recognition. "Beeeee," you murmured with wonder, gazing at yourself. Then, "Ef," you said when I made an *F*. And "Ay" and "Eeeee."

This kid's a prodigy, reading at two! This kid is my godson.

Perhaps in the years to come you will also forget that your baby bones were not always stalwart or so strong. You limped. No complaint. You seemed to take this particular develop- ment for granted. But you began to favor one leg over the other, and walking became a difficulty.

In fact, it was on a Sunday morning that I first became aware of trouble. Your leg came too close to my coffee cup; I shifted it, and you whispered, "Ow," so fleetingly—but then without a sound you started to cry. You gazed at me with a sort of pleading through the tears that shined in your Brandon eyes, and I saw again that astonishing trust. You trusted your godfather somehow to help. Oh, Baby B, how could I? I didn't know what hurt you. Too deep. The trouble was hidden too deeply in your tiny body.

But your parents were ahead of me. They had already planned to take you to the doctor.

And this is a thing I hope you will forget completely: the X-rays revealed a growth high in your leg, near the hip, against the thighbone.

Your mother and father listened as the doctor enumer- ated the possible problems, from a cyst to a malignancy. Then he explained which procedures he would advise. But his language was indirect and faintly patronizing. He described "windows" into your leg—until your mother fixed him with a baleful eye and said, "If you don't want a hysterical mother here, you'd better speak clearly to me." The doctor blinked and began in a more respectful tone to use the word "biopsy."

You have bold parents, B. They are patient and faithful. Their patience may—as with silly physicians and sillier children—come sometimes to an end. But never their faith.

They said to the doctor, "Yes, schedule a biopsy. Schedule a biopsy. But we, in the meantime—we will pray for our son."

We all prayed for you, then, Brandon Michael Piper. You won't remember. But the aunts and the uncles, your parents and grandparents and godparents and the whole congregation of Grace commended to heaven both your big name and your little leg.

Someone worried about the intensity of your parents' praying. He said, "But what if the boy's too sick? What if he doesn't get well? Doesn't it scare you that you might lose your faith if God doesn't answer the prayer?"

But your parents said, "We will pray for our son."

You see, Brandon, this was their faith: not that they felt God had to heal you on account of prayer, but rather that they wanted never to stand apart from God, especially not now. Yes, they were scared for you. But they were never, never scared of God, nor ever scared to lose God. They took their Baby B to the steadfast arms of the Father so that *whatever* happened, the love of God would hold it. Might there be a healing? Then give glory to God. Must there be a worse hurt? Then let the dear Lord strengthen everyone when strength would be most needed.

Their prayer was meant neither as a demand nor as magic, neither an ultimatum nor manipulation of the Deity. It was love. It was their highest expression of faith—not faith in your healing, Brandon (though they yearned that) but faith in God.

This is an important distinction which, in the future, you must remember. Your parents' faith did not depend upon God's "correct" answer to their prayer. Instead, the reality of their prayer depended upon their faith. With prayer they encircled you as tightly as you do hug my neck on Sunday mornings—and behold: that circle of faith was the arm of the Almighty.

And then there came the night when you could not sleep because of the pain. You cried, not silently this time. You broke your mama's heart. So that was when the patience of your parents (but not their faith!) came to an end. They bundled you to the hospital, and the biopsy which had been scheduled too many weeks in the future was immediately rescheduled.

Dear Brandon, whatever else you forget in the future, remember this: God loves you.

I was there, my godson, when they signed the love of God upon you—as if God himself wrote his name across your forehead, saying *I own this one; this one is mine.* I was there when they gave you *your* sober, senatorial name, and it became the name of you forever. I was there when they washed you thrice with a purging water, and I with my own ears heard them say, "Brandon Michael Piper, I baptize you in the name of the Father, and of the Son, and of the Holy Spirit." That's how I became your godfather. That's how the mighty God became your own most holy Father, your final Father after all. That's how the magnificent name of *Brandon Michael* got written into the Book of Life. And that, child, was a healing for any hurt which you shall ever encounter, because it has overcome death itself.

Of course your parents would not lose faith if you weren't healed of this particular problem in your thighbone. They might be very sad for you, but they would not despair— because your baptism had already declared the rising of all your bones in the end.

Whatever else you do in the future, Brandon, hold to the God that now holds you. Pray always as your parents prayed for you. Cling to the body of Jesus more tightly than you do to mine on Sunday mornings. And the God who signed you will love you infinitely, finer, and longer than ever I could—

As it happened, the biopsy proved the growth benign. It shall be removed, together with all memory of a falling limp and the nighttime pain.

And I will continue, Brandon Michael Piper, a little longer to let you sleep on my shoulder in church. But you will grow. You'll pull back from such dependencies upon earthly fathers, godfathers first, flesh fathers second. Even then I will pray for you, my godson, my Baby B.

And this shall be my prayer: that you never pull back from the God who, since your baptism, is your Father forever

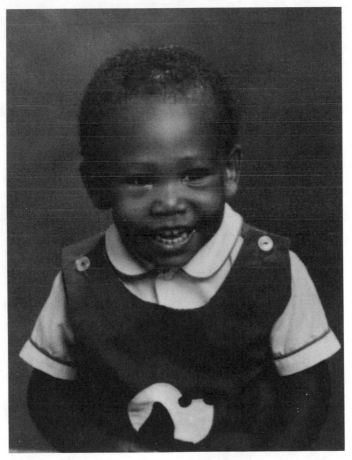

Baby B

10

An Instruction: The Difference Between Punishment and Discipline

Should the parent punish or discipline the child?

Prisons punish. By most accounts, that's all they can do. Some parents punish too, but that's not all *we* can do, nor is it what we're charged by God to do. Nor is it healthy.

Rather, it was for discipline that we were set above the children and the children under us.

Punishment administers pain for pain and hurt for hurt. If it is meted in an ethical manner, it makes the pain the criminal gets equal the pain he gave. It balances the social books of righteousness. And if it loves anything, it loves the law. Or vengeance. Or, at its best, society as a whole. But it does not love the criminal. Simply, he is made to pay *post factum* the debt his crime incurred; and the social order is, by an eye and an eye, a tooth and a tooth, preserved. Society receives the benefit. Except that he will be restrained hereafter, the criminal is scarcely affected or changed: correctional facilities do precious little correcting.

On a level more rude, punishment is merely the expression of someone's discontent, irritation, anger—and then nothing is loved so much as that one's thwarted desires and his own power to say so. Again, nothing changes.

But discipline loves the criminal.

And though discipline also gives pain, unlike punishment it seeks to change the child at the core of his being.

Note, please: the benefit of punishment is for the person or the system administering punishment; but the benefit of discipline is for the one who is *being* disciplined. It is, says the writer to the Hebrews, "for his good, that he may share in holiness." A supernatural benefit!

Moreover, it is a gift of the discipliner to the disciplined, both of whom will suffer the pain of the process: "For the moment all discipline seems painful rather than pleasant; later it yields the peaceful fruit of righteousness to those who have been trained by it." But if a parent says that the pain is "for your own good, you little ——," and punishes to relieve himself—for anger's sake or for vengeance or because he's lost control, but in no wise to plant in his child *the peaceful fruit of righteousness*—he lies in his teeth, committing a double treachery and multiple sins in a single swat.

Does the parent seek tears? It is punishment. Does the parent grow frustrated when there are no tears? When there is no sign of pain? It is punishment.

And punishment is not the charge God gave the parents.

Another difference: discipline is an extended and carefully managed event, not a sudden, spontaneous, personal reaction to the child's behavior.

I sat with a mother in her kitchen, visiting. Her daughter toddled in, whining, and yanked the woman's skirt.

"Don't. We're talking," said her mother. She gave the kid a cookie and continued to talk.

But the cookie lasted only a little while. When it was eaten, the child was back, whining again and yanking her mother's skirt.

"I said don't!" She nudged the kid and kept talking.

A third yank earned a vague wave of the hand.

The fourth yank earned a swat on the butt.

And when the child began truly to cry, the mother in exasperation stood up, hoisted the girl, and hauled her from the room. "When will she ever learn?" she said. She punished the kid by dumping her in her crib and closing the bedroom door.

"Punished," I say, because this was in no way a careful event for the child's sake, in love with the child. It was altogether for the parent's desire, peace, and ease.

An event. . . .

Let Jesus teach us.

Even as he disciplined Simon Peter, so may we discipline our children—seeking, as he did Peter's, the children's righteousness that they might share in holiness.

The end of such a process is that they know the love of God and their place within it.

It has three steps and a peaceful response to the child's sin. She is of our flesh and we are sinners. She is not different from us. Therefore—

1. Anticipate the sin

Right clearly and with sufficient sadness to indicate the wrong, Jesus said, "You will deny me, even before the rooster crows the morning in." He didn't argue it. He said it. He prepared Peter to recognize the sin when it would occur—for he couldn't change Peter's soul if the sin had never surfaced, nor could he change Peter's mind if the disciple didn't see and acknowledge the sin when it did.

It must be the same for the parents. Choose a few significant rules to be kept in your household (not countless numbers, stirred up by your own continual frustration in the face of having kids around). Choose rules that touch upon the child's deepest righteousness. Consider the two most elemental commandments: loving God, loving others. Let your rules define *this* behavior in the child.

Declare them clearly. Post them if necessary so that the child surely is aware of them. There is no need to argue them. They are not here to restrain the child right now (for our own peace) but for training her when she breaks the rule.

She will break the rule.

That, in fact, is the point. It's her nature. It's the "Adam," the "Eve" you seek to change by discipline. If you anticipate the transgression as much in your emotions (peacefully), as in your planning (this is just step 1), you won't explode at the sin ("You rotten kid! Oh, where did I go wrong?"). Rather, you will be glad that her sinful nature surfaced and gave you the opportunity to teach and revise it. Also, you won't act in anger (punishment) but will in cool love discharge the duty God gave you as a parent.

2. In the very instant of the sin, shine a light on it

Call it wrong and painful to others and self-destructive.

Peter did, of course, deny the Lord exactly as the Lord had said, exactly as the Lord expected. In that instant two things happened: the cock crowed to remind Peter of Jesus' prediction, to apply the name of the sin which Jesus had given it earlier, to persuade Peter that Jesus was, in fact, superior. Peter could not *not* see himself as Jesus had seen him now. He had not kept his promise: "If I must die with you, I will not deny you." Jesus was right (so Peter knows by the predicted rooster crow) and Peter was wrong.

Moreover, in the moment of his denial, Jesus "turned and looked at him." The sin was not antiseptic. It was very personal. It hurt someone whom Peter loved. And Peter must see that in Jesus' wounded eyes. This is *shining a light* on the sin. This is, in the same gesture, shining a light on the sinner. Peter saw himself more clearly now than he had when he boasted.

He went out and wept bitterly.

The pain he caused in someone else is the pain he felt in

himself (this is what guilt—a good thing!—accomplishes), so for Peter sin was no longer an abstract concept, but an act both real and dangerous and his own. His personal pain communicates better than any argument, any rational discourse. Such awareness comes in experience.

Let it be the same for the parents. When your child breaks the rule, immediately communicate the wrongness of the act and its painful consequences and the child's responsibility for it. In terms she can understand, define it for her. Speak to both her mind and her soul that she and you—the both of you—have been wounded.

In a special place of the house (rooms define our actions) by a repeated and recognized ritual (for she shall not sin once, but often) name the rule again and mark the details of her breaking it (as Jesus used the rooster to remind Peter of what he'd said in the past). *Do you remember, child? This is the rule. And this is what you did. Do you remember both, child?* So and so: the sin as a sin becomes real unto her in the conversation of your relationship.

Do none of this in anger. Be sad. You love her. You can survive as you are, but she must change for her survival. You have been hurt. Now the hurt must communicate itself to her. For finally it is not your hurt but the child's of which she must be persuaded. Therefore, (ah, me!) let pain define both the general effect of sin and the kid's responsibility—and the ultimate personal suffering of that effect (for destruction circles back, in the end, upon the destroyer). What she feels will speak to her more than rational discourse: you may (though many may not) choose a careful spanking.

"Careful." Act *after* you've named the sin and reminded the child of its consequence—not immediately or passionately.

"Careful." Adhere to the consequence prescribed for any infraction. If it's two weeks' grounding, keep to two weeks, no more, no less. If it's five swats, then let it be five swats, no more for anger, no less for tenderness.

"Careful." Any spanking must hurt the parent equally to the child. A flat hand on a covered butt. Flesh absolutely must feel flesh. I mean that no instrument can come between to increase one's pain and decrease the other's. And there can be no true wound. It is the tactile communication the parent seeks, not punishment. Not punishment. No, not punishment.

And this parent will recognize her love in her own pain. If there is no parental pain, there must be no such discipline. Choose something else!

3. Heal the hurt

This must follow or else what you have done is merely punishment.

Please read John 21:15–19.

After the sin Jesus took time and patience to repair the relationship between himself and Peter. More than that, he called Peter to greater faithfulness and mightier action, proving his trust both in the strength of his (Jesus') forgiveness to change the man and in the reality of his (Peter's) change. Thrice Peter had denied the Lord; thrice, therefore, did the Lord ask him to declare his love (and by the third declaration Peter clearly saw the effect of his sin, because he was grieved—reminded and grieved); and thrice Jesus showed confidence in Peter's ministry thereafter, in Peter's worth, in Peter: "Feed my lambs. Tend my sheep. Feed my sheep." *All is well,* the Lord Jesus said by repeating then the words with which he had called Peter in the first place: "Follow me."

All is well.

Once again let it be the same for the parents. There are three necessary gestures at this point, all modeled upon Jesus' gentle ministrations.

When the child's tears subside, speak again the sin in such a way that your love is proven unchanged; speak again the rule that had been broken; speak again the child's personal responsibility in breaking it—but cast your entire talk in the gentlest of terms: love, love—"Do you love me?" Jesus asked in order to give Peter opportunity to prove that he no longer denies but loves.

The sin is not hidden now or else forgotten; you do want

the child to change, to move beyond this iniquity, and so you both must from a new vantage confront it. But love outlives the sin and its consequence.

Next, touch the child. Physically. As physically you communicated her wrong, communicate your love. Touch her now not for pain but for gentleness and in soft caress. The touch communicates. Hold her. Hug her. This is critical for finally changing her. Tell her her worth and your abiding, unchanging affection.

Finally, affirm her worth (and prove your renewed trust in her) by giving her specific responsibilities in the household, as Jesus right easily called Peter back into discipleship: *Feed my sheep.* Make the responsibility real, something which, if she does it well, benefits others—benefits *you!*

If you punish only, the spanking shall have satisfied you and there you cease—abusing your kid. If you discipline, this loving satisfies her need for spiritual growth, for it announces her share in holiness, her newness, and your trust.

Now, love is not flaccid.

Parents are not appointed to be the buddies of their children, seeking their affections and praise, seeking ever and ever to keep the kid happy. Parents, rather, are called to be instruments of God for the children, seeking their holiness.

Love does not neglect to discipline. That's negligence. But neither is love the plain demand for obedience by pain. That's punishment.

If we love our children as the Father loves us, that is parenting indeed.

11

Joe's Nose

*P*oor Joseph!

He's got an aggressive schnoz on him.

A blade. A dorsal fin with which to cut the air. A nose of royal proportion.

I don't mean Joseph of the many-colored dream-coat or Stalin or Joe DiMaggio or furious McCarthy. Not Chief Joseph of the Nez Percé; no, nor the holy Roman emperors who numbered themselves as Josephs first and second.

I mean my kid.

Let this be a warning to children in general:

NEVER SCORN YOUR PARENTS!
FOR WHAT THEY ARE, THOU SHALT BECOME.
THY SCORN SHALL DESCEND ON THYSELF
IN THE END.

God gave this mostly gentle Joseph, son of our love, an aptitude for drawing. He has ever had an eye for detail and a hand to sketch the sight on paper. He learned both watercolor and acrylic/oil painting early from a woman who loved and honored him. Mary Ellen Philips tutored him in her own home.

But the pleasure of his personal interest was cartooning.

Even in grade school this kid could caricature a teacher with such wicked precision—catching the right quirk and exaggerating it—that everyone knew straightway who it was and why she was silly. Joe saw the small iniquity that set a person apart from others; Joe drew the bloop that made her funny.

And the folks who saw his drawings wept with laughter. He has a crack-shot sense of humor.

But he himself has never laughed much. Joseph maintains a mostly droll and seemingly indifferent expression, curling the corner of his lip in ironic smiling. Raising a single eyebrow. Detached, as it were.

Nevertheless, inside himself the world looks weird, and he can picture that weirdness in pencil-drawings with a swift, devastating accuracy. God might repent having given the kid the gift, since the gift is a weapon of sorts; but he has it now, and he can't contain it. He draws fools foolish. Silliness becomes as prominent as a three-hair wart on a preacher's nose. And hypocrisies, by the pencil of my son, are stripped away, revealing the bone beneath the skin, the sin beneath the smile.

And so it came to pass one year that Joseph and I drove down to Kentucky, to a cabin on Lake Beshear, just south of Dawson Springs.

He was approaching the hairless edge of puberty.

I planned to talk about sex.

Thanne and I had decided to give our children, one by one, a private weekend each, in which privacy (before the hormones knocked the body stupid) we would discuss sexuality and baby making and maturity and genuine love and so forth.

Joseph, the oldest, was first. (I got the boys, Thanne got the girls.) It was October. Autumn winds were stripping trees of leaves. Across the lake the forest was fire all along the shore-line, red and yellow and furious oranges, umber so dark I could die. We spent a Friday evening talking of nothing important, playing games, eating a good meal, sleeping.

Saturday morning I took him out on the lake in an outboard motorboat. Great speed. We left a sweeping wake behind us. We investigated islands no one lived on. I drove, hands at the wheel, crouching forward, somewhat tense, worried about the amount of gasoline left, a pipe clenched in my teeth.

Saturday afternoon we walked through the forest, discussing the hot topics, the cause of our coming. He was quiet, mostly. Bemused, I think. When I had pretty much finished my speech, he told me that the fourth-grade teacher had already destroyed in him any plan to bear by sexual (physical and messy) encounter. He thought that adoption would be easier than the strange engagement of body parts. He (it seemed) intended to set *me* straight about baby making and maturity and genuine love and so forth.

Joseph! Adult from the get-go!

And talented.

That Saturday night he found paper and pencil and drew a cartoon:

Me in profile, gripping the wheel of a speedboat, a long-stemmed pipe clenched in my teeth, the pipe boiling forth an enormous smoke—

—and a nose on my face like the fin of a fish, a nose of magnificent size, straight, aggressive, nostrils flaring, a forehead swept back and an eye both bright and tiny and intense.

Poor Joseph!

The caricature was, in fact, hilarious.

It was perfectly accurate: I could not deny my grim silliness, my manner of attack for things that scare me (like talking to my son of sexuality, like wondering whether a boat has gas enough to get us home again). All such passive-aggression he drew into that nose. That single explosive nose. A nose of marvelous *Forward Ho!*-ing. Oh, my son: he laughed at me without cracking a smile. He reduced me to the stupid bone of what, indeed, I am.

And now he is growing up.

Poor Joseph!

The caricature is of himself.

We are now together at Valparaiso University, my son and I. He has just returned from a semester's study in Germany (and from all the travel thereunto attendant).

I teach at Valparaiso.

But I *am* here, and the kid can't cancel that. Worse, I am *here* and the kid can scarcely stand that.

For what he said of me when I was young and he was younger has likewise come to pass for him, now that he's an adult whose nose has grown to its final finny size.

He is becoming his father. The same one whom earlier he had severed from himself by pencil and quick criticism. But he had severed himself from his real self.

For now the kid bears the nose he mocked ten years ago.

It's a kick in the head, isn't it? That which you considered silly in your parents is, precisely, yourself.

The forth commandment is not an accident: it was offered in love for you! Honor your father and your mother, that it may be well with you.

For if you dishonor them by any sundering means, by any superiority for their dim-witted and ancient notions, you shall, in the end, take honor from your *self*.

Love your parents, children.

They are your present and your future.

They are you.

And the best way *you* may live long in the land is by keeping them there. See?

12

Little Lamb,
Who Made Thee?

Secretly beaten.

Sexually abused—

O child, it's not your fault. You do not have to earn the approval of your tormentor—no, nor his forgiveness either!

Is it strange that a victim thinks she caused the wrong and must right it again? Well, not so strange when we consider her helplessness. She's looking for leverage. She needs some principle by which to control her horror. And if *her* sin caused the punishment, then *she* might prevent it by a confession. See?

So the victim seeks her own iniquity—and the Christian faith is made grotesque thereby, allowing the guiltless to suffer guilt. And the abuser's become a Destroyer therefore, both of the body and the soul.

No, child—it was his act.

He was its cause. He was its doer. He took the wretched benefit. He must own it now, not you, not you.

He did it!

But because of your native innocence (which your tormentor encourages, since it shifts his guilt to you), and because you crave order in dangerous chaos (some ethical order anyway), you see a connection between one's behavior and one's fate. The good get goodness back again; and the bad get hurt—and look what a mess you're in; therefore you must be bad. Is that how you think? It saves the world from absurdity, doesn't it? It argues a certain rationality in human affairs. Good is rewarded, evil is punished, right? And your punishment proves evil in yourself, right? *WRONG!* Absolutely, unequivocally wrong.

✓ If you've suffered abuse, the one who abused you sinned.

Sin is an uncaused evil. Responsibility sticks with the sinner. The sin came from him. He is the source. He bears the blame. His is the shame. Not you! Not yours! Do you hear me?

You, my child; you, dear lamb—you are beautiful and clean.

This sin occurred because a fool considered himself superior to you. He considered his whim superior to your health, his desire superior to your body, his mood superior to your peace. But you were made in the image of God, so his action condemns him: he demeans the creature whom God exalted; he attacks the child whom heaven loves. Listen: such spiritual blindness, such bestial selfishness, such a pitiful lack of self-control, declares this fool your inferior after all. You needn't seek kindness from him. Rather, he can't continue to live without your forgiveness. *He needs you!*

But his is the more desperate state, because right now you need do nothing for him. No, no, you may withhold forgiveness until (1) you have regained a genuine wholeness again after his savagery, and (2) he has ceased to blame you, and has sincerely recognized his sin, and has acknowledged the guilt, and has confessed aloud his ruinous guilt, and has confessed before God the bloody treachery of his guilt.

Somewhere the sin must stop!

The sinner tells me that it was his parents' fault in the first place. His father did him the same way. His mother was silent and critical. He didn't (he tells me) have a chance. He can't help his breeding and his personal shaping.

But if this is true, then we're all a cosmic landfill for every sin that ever occurred; they fall on us from the past generations, all the way back to Cain. Such a weight of sin (everyone else's fault except our own) must crush our innocent souls. Such an undeserved history must kill us.

But it hasn't killed us. In other words, there must be some break in this chain of responsibility, sinners causing sinner to sin—abusive parents turning their children into abusive parents.

And there is: it is the acceptance of responsibility *by the sinner,* by none other than the sinner himself, so that when divine forgiveness transfigures that one, the sin and the sinning are canceled together, and the chain breaks.

No, sir, it doesn't do to blame another, neither the parents before you nor the child behind you. You, sir, as perpetrator of a vile abuse, must with a contrite heart confess.

And you, the child whom he ravaged, must not call yourself ugly. You aren't. His action does not define you.

You, child: you are as soft as the blue sky. Touch your cheek. Do you feel the weft of life there? Yes: God wove you more lovely than wool of the clouds, smoother than petals of lily, sweeter than amber honey, brighter than morning, kinder than daylight, as gentle as the eve. Listen to me! You are beautiful. You are beautiful. If you think you're ugly, you've let a fool define you. Don't! Touch your throat. It is a column of wind and words. Stroke your forehead. Thought moves through its caverns. Imagination lives in there. You are the handiwork of the Creator. You are his best art, his poem, his portrait, his image, his face—and his child.

And if the Lord God took thought to create you, why would you let a sinner define you?

God caused the stars to be, and then bent low to make you.

God wrapped himself in space as in an apron, then contemplated the intricacy of your hands; he troweled the curve of your brow; he fashioned the tug of your mouth and the turn of your tongue; he jeweled your eye; he carved your bones as surely as he did the mountains.

God conceived of time and in that instant considered the purposeful thump of your heart—and the blink of your eyelid.

God made galaxies and metagalaxies, the dusty infinitude of the universe—then filled your mind with dreams as with stars.

You are not an accident. You were planned. You are the cunning intention of almighty God. Well, then, shall you think ill of yourself? NO! You shall think as well of yourself as you do of any marvel of the Deity.

Please, my sister, do not allow a sinner to steal you from yourself. You are too rare. No matter what filth has befouled you, your soul is unique in the cosmos. There is none like you. Whatever thing you admire—a leaf, a little cup, a sunset—you are more beautiful.

Sleep peacefully, you. God loves you. And so do I. And so ought you in the morning light, when the dew is a haze of blue innocence. But sleep now, child, in perfect peace. You are God's—and he spreads his wings above you now.

Part III

The Parent of His Children

The Wangerin family: Walter, Matthew, Joseph, Thanne, Talitha, and Mary
Photo credit Ralph St. Louis 1978

13

At the Child's Intrusion, His Father's Complaint

Between two fingers her nipple appears
like a searching tongue,
two dots of a blue milk printing the tip of it
while her full hand cups the breast.

Oh, how obedient is the breast
that spills around that hand!

She has bent her head and tipped it sideways,
gazing at the intimacy exposed.
Her hair like a black rain breaks at the ear,
pouring on the forehead of the baby,
the babe: the boy in the crook of her arm.

How full is her face with the face of the child!
How full is her bosom for him!

And I think her lips are fuller, too,
rolling outward in a pout.
And the air must be richer;
she breathes it so deeply;
the air in her nostrils must sparkle with gladness,
because she distends them for each inhalation,
reaching, reaching,
seizing the sweet breath—Oh!

When he cries, the baby curves his tongue
like a spoon, the rim quivering.
Oh, that muscle!
That tough, utilitarian tool,
careless of this most private flesh of my wife
which has no bone nor force to fight for itself—

Little truck driver! That is no
dashboard knob to yank at!

But she cuts pigeon sounds in her throat,
and the infant leans and takes her nipple and tugs it,
smacking the sweet milk,
sinking his eyes,
and sighing all in the small of his nose.

And so does she
yield long and light blue sighs—

while I feel alien. Never
did the woman spill so willingly for me.

14

Snowbound

*I*t was the snowfall of '76 (though I confess I'm fuzzy on dates and it might have been in '77).

January. The children were small, four of them, ages two to six. We lived in the country on two acres with chickens and fruit trees and large gardens. We were bordered by woods on the east and the south; to the west lay a farmed field; we shared the northern border with a neighbor who kept horses.

To this day the children remember a beautiful mare who slipped into a ditch and broke her leg. She had to be shot. They were the ones who discovered the accident. They stood at the edge of the ditch and watched the poor beast whinnying, lying like an eighteen-wheeler on her side, throwing her head up as if to snap her great body upright, rolling her eye so that the white showed terror.

This was new and horrible for my four young ones. Horses should not be helpless. Hugeness should not lie down and die. They came to the house with a look of awe in their faces. And then we heard the gunshot.

But that was a summer sometime after the winter of '76.

And that winter was kinder altogether, bequeathing unto us a snowfall of memorial proportions. It shut down the city for a week. Us it kept isolated for a full two weeks.

The storm began as a true blizzard, wind and a straking of snow straight out across the land. Our house leaked air, so it whistled and shuddered all night long. The boys, the older of the four, kept their eyes wide open. They had high, piping voices in those days. I heard them talking off and on about the relative strengths and weaknesses of the house.

"Joe? Joe? Is it goin' t'blow the baf-room away?"

"No, Matt, 'cause how would we pee then?"

"Oh."

By morning the wind had relented, but the snowfall itself continued down and down, and the world was utterly white. Cloaked, Siberian, forgiven. (*Though your sins be as scarlet, they shall be white as snow*). All the ruddy, rotting colors of an exhausted autumn, all the blackened, unraked leaves, the shivering stalks in the beanfield, the corrupted melons in my garden—all was covered in a smooth white purity.

The children knelt at the window, transfixed.

God had called forth a new Eden.

"Can we," they whispered.

Their tiny voices were hushed by holy things. It sounded as if they were praying.

"Can we go . . . out?"

Going out, of course, was not without danger. Pigeon Creek snaked through the woods east and south on its way to the city. Hunters prowled the wooded banks, banging at living things. Not in January, though. Other months, other days. One once mistook my dog for something wild and free.

And once, after the creek had—in a quick succession—

first flooded and then frozen, the boys snuck into the woods to explore the dazzling ice-world.

That afternoon their mother in her kitchen slowly became conscious of a distant sound, a faint cry, a sort of creaturely squeaking like fox kittens caught: "Mommy?" one voice mewed. "Mommy, mommy, mommy!"

The other voice barked, "Mop!"

Well, in those days Matthew was testing toughness. Tough kids don't say Mommy, and he never got the hang of Mom.

MOP!

Thanne ran down the hill and into the wood and found her sons stranded on a single circle of ice fixed like a tutu round the trunk of a large tree. The flood had begun to retreat. The rest of the ice, hollowed now, had broken under the boys' weight. "Mop?" They genuinely thought they would drown, tender adventurers paying for their boldness. Who knows how long they stood on the frost-island, crying?

But that was another year, another time.

Now they gazed upon a white paradise, soft, untroubled, a bosom mounded, maternal, abundant. Lo, as far as the eye could see through textured air the silent snow still coming down, the world was religious in serenity.

"Can we go ... out?"

My chickens found the drifts impossible to negotiate, too deep for their legs, too high for flight. The effort defeated them. They were plumped here and there like marshmallows in milk, their wings having made angel-wings in the snow at their sides. If I had not myself gone forth, booted and gloved and blowing clouds, to bear them back to the coop, and if I had not then shut the door against their next escape (well, to them it was day, and day demanded foraging, and the instant they were returned to the dry coop they forgot the trouble with snows), they would have starved and frozen and died.

"Dad? Dad, can we?"

"What?"
"You know—go out?"
"Why?"
"To play."

In that same blizzard of '76 certain cattle were caught out in the fields, enduring alone the long night and the terrific blowing cold. They turned their backs to the wind; they packed themselves side-by-side together; they drooped their great heads. By morning the hoarfrost of their breathing had grown big and joined the earth, trapping their snouts in heavy columns of ice. Such silent, obedient monuments, bowed down, locked to the frozen ground, patiently dying.

But that was far west of us, out on the plains. Cattle in Southern Indiana are always closer to barns; and children are safe. The children are safe. Their parents protect them and keep them safe.

"Well, can we, Dad? Is it okay to go out and play?"

My oldest son ran away from home once. He slipped out the back door and headed west on a dusty road. He got as far as the bridge over the creek. A neighbor spotted him and drove him home again. He said afterward that he was looking for us because we had left and left him with an uncle who truly frightened him—so he lit out, though he was only four years old.

Even the little ones know of danger. And I think they suspect that something like death can descend on the living. They can be frightened. Their parents, of course, do more than suspect. Parents know in the cold part of their hearts that children can die.

"Yes," I said. "Yes, you can go out to play."

Grins bloomed in four faces, four little foxes whose

expressions should never freeze in fierce grimaces—no, not these bounding and beautiful kittens.

"Wait!" I said. "Wait for me!"

Oh, my children, my children, so wonderfully young that winter! Oh, the radical magic of your innocence! In those days what you did *not* know transfigured the world I *did* know into something generous and kind and joyful and motherly and good after all.

This, then, is what I recall of the snows of '76: that we stomped a huge pie in a white field and chased each other down trails three feet deep and fell and laughed and blew clouds in frigid air and no one was hurt.

I remember snow forts in our snowbound days, each fort confronting the other, and snowballs stacked like cannonballs, and dusty throws of soft ammunition, and no one was hurt, and everyone felt the safety and the dearness of family.

I remember an ache in my wrist from the snow that crammed my mittens.

I remember an ache in my heart.

There was a snowman so huge that both my sons could stand on his hips to have their picture taken, their arms spread out like Hollywood stars, laughing, fearing nothing.

We ice-skated on Pigeon Creek.

For two full weeks we went out and played every day. And I loved my children until I wept. And not one of them was wounded. Not one.

But that was a very long time ago.

15

No Fields of Yellow Flowers Anymore

i.

When our neighbor informed us that our small son could no longer play with her daughter, I was sorry, but I didn't argue. Rather, I took the opportunity to school him in self-restraint.

Even from infancy Matthew had been an exuberant child. Life and every desire were matters of gladness for him. He was up with the morning sun, loud and laughing and out the door, racing the fields like a sheepdog, loving the grass and the speed and the freedom. Oh, Matthew! He was three and free—never, never the slave of anyone or of anything.

We lived in the country in those days. I raised all sorts of fruits and vegetables. Matthew tended to the sweeter crop always—and when strawberries fattened in the green patch, he did not, as he said, "Think two times." He flew on wings of an aching hunger faster than anyone else, landing on hands and knees, ramming his face among the leaves.

I yearned to delight in life as he did.

At the same time I wished that he would learn self-discipline because he could hurt himself. He could hurt others, too—and he did, and he always felt remorse thereafter, and that was perhaps the worst way of hurting himself, but he did it again. He always did it again.

Ah, the wild child! There was such a splendid joy in his satisfactions. Unrestrained in action, he was also unrestrained in gladness—and then again as unrestrained in sadness when his natural self would wound another. It all went together, you see? Desire and delight and a native skill gave Matthew the edge: so he got there first; he ate it first; he at it *all,* thinking of nothing but the fat red strawberry bursting its sugarjoy against his palate—until there was none left for others. Nothing for his family. Nothing for his three-year-old friend, who may have felt frightened by such energies both going and coming.

So, then, I didn't argue when her mother announced the new rule: "Your son is out of control," she said, and she ended the friendship. The children were forbidden to visit. No more playing. No talking, no whispering secrets. Nothing.

Matthew was suddenly very sad when I told him this law. He really liked the girl, this tiny porcelain person so different from himself, small-boned, wispy-haired, blue veins in a milk-white skin. His eyes grew large and silent in sadness, and I took the opportunity to teach:

"You've got to think of other people first, Matthew," I said, "or look what happens. People go away." We stood in our backyard, he gazing across the new, invisible wall, I gazing down at him. "Matthew, give before you take. Walk before you run. Listen before you talk, and whisper before you shout."

But he kept gazing next door.

He murmured, "Now but she don't have a friend too, either."

"I guess not," I said.

"My fault," he whispered.

I held my peace.

He looked up at me. "Daddy, can I take her a bowl of strawberries?" *Daddy, can I fix the friendship?*

"Not now," I said. "We don't have any ripe strawberries left, remember?"

He kept looking at me. "Well, maybe later," I said, thinking that Matthew's lesson might honestly change him, and the change in him might change our neighbor's mind. Maybe she'd relax her law in the future.

I was wrong on every count. Worse: I was deceived, and when the truth appeared I saw in it the dangerous intransigence of the imagination of the human heart.

Within the month my wife telephoned me at the office. "Come home," she said. She was crying. Thanne seldom cried. "Please come home right now," she said. "I found out why Mrs. Duvall cut Matthew off from her daughter—"

"Because he's hyperactive," I said.

"Please," Thanne sobbed, "just come home."

I did. I drove home. I listened for ten minutes to Thanne's explanation, hearing how wrong I could be. My blood rose up in fury. I went straightway to the house of our neighbor and, with restraint, confronted her. She answered in civil voice. In fact, she spoke in a smiling conspiratorial tone, as if two intelligent adults such as ourselves would agree on a matter like this. She felt no need to explain nor to apologize— no, not even to feel guilty. But Thanne's information had been absolutely accurate. And the way this woman accepted so serenely my burning accusation, the complete ignorance of any wickedness in all of this, astonished and aggrieved me— which dead-sorrow of soul I have not forgotten even to this day.

I came home and looked for my son. I found him downhill behind the house in a field full of yellow flowers, his arms flung out to some interior melody, turning circles. Actually, the flowers were a kind of weed in poor soil, profuse that summer; but to me they seemed most terribly beautiful for that my son was in their midst, and my heart was smitten thereby. The yellow field seemed a sort of grounded sunlight, a glory around his dark complexion.

Oh, Matthew!

I descended to him, then knelt in the field, and gathered the boy in a hug so tight he grunted.

"Daddy? Daddy, what's the matter?"

"Well, let's keep our strawberries here. We'll eat them together. But I don't think we should take them next door. Not now. Not ever."

Matthew had huge brown eyes. "Why?" he said. "Don't they like strawberries?"

He didn't understand. Nor, at that age, could he. In time he would, of course; but then he would be more than sad. The boy would be confused and wounded personally; and by then he'd know that he was suffering the assaults of a most iniquitous world.

ii.

Parents, we teach our children fairness; and we do well.

The selfish child is a danger. The self-centered child grows into a marauding adult whose sins are justified by that same grim idol, *Self.*

We wish our children to be good, and so we teach them to be just; to be selfless themselves; to do to others as they would have others do unto them. We teach them to be fair.

We do well.

And we do it (don't we?) out of deep parental fears and affections. We train them in fairness for their own protection, because we do not want them to suffer blame or slaps hereafter, do we? In a world both bigger and badder than they are, selfish children are dangerous mostly to themselves.

So we take every opportunity to say: "Don't be selfish. Share with your friends, and they will stay friends with you." Cause and effect, right? While buttoning their coats for school, we say, "Play by the rules, kid, and others will learn to trust you. They will *like* the one who knows right from wrong and acts upon it." Connections, right? Good people do good;

good invites good friends; goodness gets goodness in return. We drive our youth to college, repeating the fine and fundamental ethic: "Be fair, son, even when I'm not near to watch you. O my dear daughter, out of your own soul, be fair. This is moral independence. This is maturity. When you practice fairness, you are on your own finally and surely. Be fair."

In this way we imply that they have a personal control over their destinies: certain behaviors will have certain consequences. Choose the right behavior for a righteous future. All we teach them is based upon the presumption that there is a reasonable law at work in the world—reasonable and feasible and universal and impartial: *The Law of Fairness.*

Its positive expression is this: Good behavior earns a good reward. Good gets goodness in return. This is a most consoling logic, both for the parent and the child.

Its neutral expression is: If you do not misbehave, you will be left in peace.

And its negative: But if you break the law, the world will punish you according to your deserving. Ill deeds bring an ill response. This may be a cold logic, but it is orderly withal and necessary.

The Law of Fairness does not pretend to love people; rather, it loves stability in the community, and everyone benefits. It maintains a structure that all can understand, within which every individual can choose good or evil for himself. Its very rigidity, therefore, permits a moral liberty person by person, gives ethical independence to child and child, no child excepted.

See? In any game—in this game particularly—it's good that there are rules, and good to know the rules, and good that the referees are watching the rules. Each individual may now play heartily, and the winner *is* a winner after all.

So we teach our children *The Law of Fairness* as carefully as we can, both to know it and to obey it. And we do well thereby; and all should *be* well therefore.

And all *would* be well—if the world itself obeyed that law.

But what if the world the children encounter tears fairness to shreds? What then?

iii.

At ten-thirty on a Saturday night Matthew was just coming out of a gas station door, his head down, counting change, when he heard shouts by his car.

He looked up. Two police officers were pointing stern fingers in the faces of his friends. His friends were backpedaling, helpless.

One of the officers shouted: "Get in the car! Get in the car right now!"

This, Matthew knew, was not possible. By habit he'd hit the button that locked the doors. Even as he broke into a trot toward the gas pumps, he heard the cop continue: "Get in, boy, or you're going to jail!"

Exact quotes (though not unlike other quotes he has heard often and often). Matthew doesn't forget what he meets with emotion. His mind and his heart are strong.

He pulled the car keys from his pocket as he approached the scene. The officer saw him and redirected the order. To Matthew, now, he yelled, "Open this car. Get in and get out of here, now, *now!*—or you're the one going to jail!" Matt's the one. My son is the one.

He was seventeen years old. (But it happened when he was sixteen. It has happened every year of his driving life.) He had by then developed a flat manner for precisely this sort of situation. That is, he blanked his eyes and slacked his face and slowed all motion until nothing in him suggested threat, aggression, or flight. He stared into the air. He neither grimaced nor smiled nor said, "Sir." Any such gesture is dangerous.

Deliberately Matthew began to unlock the four doors of the car—

And the uniforms exploded: "Not fast enough. I don't like your attitude, boy! In fact, show me ID. Now, now, NOW!"

Just then a friend whom the police hadn't seen stepped round the car, surprising them. "Yow!" They both leaped backward snatching their sidearms. Embarrassed, they yelled, "Oh, yeah! Oh, yeah, you are going to jail!"

Matthew stood absolutely still, now *not* giving back what he was getting nor getting what he had ever given; now *not* invoking fairness nor anticipating it nor even believing in it— for he had learned, Lord; he had learned beyond my teaching him; he had learned that the best posture in a crisis like this is not to be. Vanish.

Matthew had learned by cruel and redundant experience.

I do not lie. I declare it as an objective fact that my son has regularly been harassed by officers of the law for no ill that he has done and in spite of the good that he has sincerely chosen.

My son is adopted.

He is black.

His color alone is, in this world, the cause of his harassment.

iv.

We live now in a black neighborhood, in the center of our city, where there is the congeniality of community for our children.

The police here are mostly white.

But we were not wrong to move here. Here most of the people suffer the same derisions of *The Law of Fairness,* and here we can talk of the trouble to folks who understand it in their bodies as well as in their minds.

While we still lived out in the country, we experienced the cold, white eye alone; and we, at first, were inclined to accept guilt. Well, we hadn't yet learned. We didn't recognize the depth of human prejudice nor the bland face it wore. We thought it was we and our children who were somehow at fault. We (Thanne and I in our own belated ignorance) were still assuming fairness to be an active principle of human relationship—

—until our neighbor spoke the truer motive of her mind.

That's why I hugged my son so hard and why he looked so terribly beautiful and tragic in the field of yellow flowers. The mother of his young friend had just said to me, without anger but with a complete and creedal conviction: "They won't never talk again 'cause black and white don't marry."

That was the reason for the separation.

She said, "I don't want them touching or holding hands or whispering secrets. It's unnatural. You go on and keep him hobbled and at home, away from my girl, 'cause black and white don't—"

don't marry, she said, when these two children were no more than three years old. And she smiled as if I would surely understand the long weight and history of her truth.

But this was truth: that *The Law of Fairness* crumbled in the face of such mindless, murderous racism.

The Law of Fairness was a far less effective ward in the wicked world than the "trick" that Matthew had learned thereafter, which is not to trust anyone, which is the blank expression, the slack face, and vanishing. Do nothing. Say nothing. Be nothing.

That night, when he was still seventeen, it worked. He seemed to the officers sufficiently subservient. He did not go to jail. He came home. He shrugged and told me the story, by then a very old story. No big deal. This is the way things are. Cops harass young black males.

But I wish he were three again, dark and lovely in a field of yellow flowers, laughing as once he laughed when he was innocent, when desire and delight and satisfaction and life were all one with him. Fairness was a good law then. And my son could hope and be happy then—

v.

All of our children must suffer the loss of that good law. Do you understand? The world is not, after all, fair.

So what do we do when it is the world and not our

children which proves selfish in the real encounter?—selfish and unrepentant and unpunished after all?

Teachers will deal unfairly with our daughters; coaches will scream at our sons, pink and popeyed; friends will trash our children at the pleasure of other friends; bosses will play favorites; the marketplace will not love our children as we do, but will rather love itself at their expense; countless promises will be made and, though the children count on them, will then be broken. Politicians will lie. Police will obey the imagination of their hearts more than the cool and equable law. So what do we do when bad people possess power while good and goodness are crushed as wimp and weakness?

Injustice, in this fallen world, will certainly strike the child both bluntly and personally.

Listen, parents:

If we do nothing, if we do no more than communicate *The Law of Fairness* strictly and only, then our children will change to protect themselves, but the change will break our hearts.

One young man may react with an anger so radical that all our teaching—all of it!—shall be compromised and lost on him. He may then mimic the world, exchanging laws of fairness for laws of brutality: might makes right. The strong survive. Look out for number one, since you have no better friend than yourself.

Or one young woman, having been deceived, may never trust another person again. To the degree that she was burned for her faith in fairness, to that same degree she shall now doubt promises altogether and dread the motives of other people. Scared child! If hurt came from the place she had considered safe, then hurt can come from anywhere. And love itself becomes the ultimate personal risk—too dangerous ever to take. Lonely child, unfulfilled and frightened.

Or the saddest change within our children is this, that they never let go of *The Law of Fairness,* that they accept therefore the guilt and consider themselves deserving of all the hurt the world gives unto them. A harsh twist: they believe themselves evil precisely because they have had to suffer evil.

And if they cannot perceive what wrong they did to cause it, soon they conclude that it is the wrong they *are*.

If, when this good law breaks in a broken world, we do nothing new for our children, they shall begin to die various early deaths.

vi.

At Bosse High School Matthew played the point position for his basketball team. He had the spirit of a leader. Even off the court he wove his players together by driving them hither and yon in his car, by giving them haircuts in our basement, by gathering the team together at our house before a game. I remember with pleasure the laughter bubbling from the basement, and I cooked suppers for them, and I felt a parent indeed.

All but two of the Bosse players were black.

I remember, too, how nervous the team would become on the days they had to be bused from the city into the counties of southern Indiana to play small-town high schools in all-white communities.

These plain folk in their own gymnasiums enjoyed a joke or two. When they met a team as black as Bosse's, their fans would enter the stands carrying hubcaps. Humor. Matthew and his teammates simply expected it. Students wore watermelon patches, red, green, and seeded. "Fun! It's all in good fun!" Yet, though he expected it, Matthew genuinely did not understand why this was considered funny, why folks laughed, why parents rocked backward on their seats amused. Oh, he knew that whites think that blacks like watermelon. But why such an unsubstantiated notion of one people regarding another should make the first people laugh, he had not a clue. But he tolerated these milder forms of foolishness. All the Bosse players did. Part of basketball. Hoosier hysteria. We live in Evansville on the Ohio River.

But then in the dark midwinter of 1988—just as the bus and its basketball team were slowing down to turn off Highway 231 into the parking lot of a rural high school—

there flared beside the windows a sudden fire, a bright ascending yellow flame. Suddenly, boys could see boys' faces in the firelight, and the bus driver gunned his engine. Matthew's eyes went as wide as when he was young. The entire team fell silent, watching.

This was the first time any of them had seen a cross afire.

Matthew (he later told me) had such tightness in his chest he couldn't breathe. It occurred to him that a fire near a high school was unsafe. Even the building might burn.

So, then, how do you exit a bus in front of strangers? How do you strip and change clothes in foreign walls? How do you enter the glaring light and loud sound of a basketball court when your own mood is so filled with confusion? Well, the act had seemed so obscene to Matthew—that someone should burn the cross of Jesus. What had Jesus done? He couldn't make sense of it. His stomach was knotted. His face felt hot. Something was dreadfully wrong. But how do you walk on court when everyone else is happy, laughing, and ordinary?— though somebody in this place just torched the wood of the Christian cross.

Well, you enter stiff. Wooden-legged. You put on the blank-eyed mask of not-caring, the impenetrable wall and the slack-faced declaration that nothing matters. You pretend indifference even while your heart ticks so quickly you feel the pulse in your throat, and your ears are so acute that they hear the whispers, *Nigger, nigger*. But the word registers nowhere in your expression. You take the ball. You shoot. Your warm up. Stretch. Avoid looking at the stands. Shoot. Shoot. Shoot.

vii.

There is another law. The laws of fairness and brutality are not the only ones a child might learn. Against these two— or against lawlessness altogether—the third is absolutely essential.

This is what we do when the children suffer the failure of fairness in the world: with all our hearts, for the health and the blessing of the children forever, we model before them and for them enact *The Law of Forgiveness*.

Parents, if we love them this is not a matter of choice. It is necessary for the life of the children. Without it, they shall be caught in a killing society, dying. Moreover, it is at the core of our Christian faith: a loving God knew the need long before we did. . . .

We who have been appointed parents by the most Holy Parent must in all our action image the forgiveness of Christ himself—and must name Christ Jesus both as the Lord and as the source of what we are doing. No secrets here. His forgiveness must pattern the children's. His forgiveness must empower theirs. And as their spirits more and more reflect the Spirit of God, they shall more and more be *free of the world*—neither to be ruled nor to be crushed by it.

This is not merely an abstract doctrine to be conned.

This is wholly pragmatic.

This is a daily shield, the children's best protection after all.

Even as we train them to eat and to dress and to perform some sustaining skill, so we must train them to sever themselves from the hurt and the powers of the world (though not from the world itself) by a true and holy pardoning.

Sinner, I do not hold this thing against you.

No, the children do not say such a thing simply on their own. They must know (by your guidance) that Jesus said it first to them from the cross, and that Jesus says it thereafter *through* them to the world before them.

Whisper their sins to their souls until they ache in sore repentance; but then quickly sing to them the measure of the mercy they have received from the dear Lord. Their sins are gone. In place of sin is righteousness and the love of God. The Spirit of love then lives within them. God is there, and from the God in them truly, truly comes this miraculous power to forgive the people who do not in fact deserve forgiveness.

But forgiving inverts the powers. Evil cannot control those who do not fear evil; and those who forgive it do not fear it; they are above it, gazing *down* upon it in pity. Nor can evil rule those who are themselves not evil. Those filled with grace are filled with God.

Children of forgiveness are liberated, therefore, from this world, utterly free, making choices altogether on their own, unpressured, unthreatened, unambitious, unpersuadable. Such children enjoy partnership with the almighty God. The world can indeed destroy *The Law of Fairness,* but it cannot destroy that which dodges its tooth, *The Law of Forgiveness.* Why, it cannot comprehend the premise at all. Forgiveness is a puzzle before it.

Again, the world can destroy any child committed to *The Law of Brutality,* since the greater power may always kill the lesser. But it cannot destroy the Holy Companion of the child of forgiveness, nor else the child that this dear Companion keeps.

And look at the marvelous accomplishments of such children of the Spirit: they become the means by which God enters the world; for their forgiveness is the coming of Jesus again and again.

Is there a higher calling than to be the bearer of the Lord?

viii.

They won. Matthew's team won.

No razzle-dazzle, no slam dunks, no show—just a steady game, a solid and solemn, respectable win. The fans in the stands were not happy.

Neither was Matthew's coach, despite the triumph. He was nervous, tense—and finally furious.

As both teams were leaving the court, a heavy-set man sitting half-way up to the ceiling bellowed something about a "nigger win," and the coach of Bosse's team blew up. With a strangled shout he began to mount risers, clearing a path by short chops of his arms, preparing to crack the skull of a fat fan who was suddenly very frightened. Friends of that fan started to converge around him, balling their fists.

But immediately both basketball teams swept up the stand together, like sea waves.

And amazingly, Matthew was not afraid. He was the first
to reach his coach. He tried to pull the short man backward
and got tossed aside for his effort. But he wasn't scared, and he
truly did not expect a fight—because of what had happened
during the game.

The first half ended in a grim stand-off, a balanced score
and an equal suspicion on both sides.

But near the beginning of the second half, Matthew (by
habit, I think, a spontaneous act) complimented his opposite
for a good shot. Just a nod, an acknowledgement between
equals: "Hey, man."

And "Hey," said his opponent.

And suddenly Matthew realized the potential of the
gesture. Several times by glances and touches he praised the
white point guard. Since he himself was known as a good
player, the compliment carried weight. And the opponent, not
bad himself, smiled back, grinned back, praised Matthew in
return.

So, then, there was a mutual relationship here, independent of the noises in the gym, shaped at first by a common
commitment to the same game. So, then, Matthew's mask
cracked and his hot face cooled. So, finally it became a
conscious gesture on his part to forgive: to honor the
humanity of the other, permitting the other as fully human
also to return relationship.

The rest of the team observed in two point guards the
lack of fear and vengefulness. They saw in Matthew a weird,
uncaused behavior (except as God causes things that otherwise
would never have happened, as God makes miracles through
his children), and so they hunkered down and played basketball. Both teams shut out the idiocy of sinful fans and
apoplectic coaches. They played the game they liked; and
within this pale of forgiveness they liked the players they
faced.

It was a good, close game.

That's why Matthew wasn't afraid when his coach arose in
a rage and he himself went after him. It was a single team that
swept up the stands and interposed itself between the Bosse

coach and the friends of a fat fan—a single team composed in equal measure of white and black players, rural and city, Bosse and Bosse's opponents.

You see? *All* the players were, by the benefaction of the forgiveness of one, perfectly free.

ix.

Yesterday I said good-bye to my son all over again. He was on his way back to college. He is twenty. I feel a heartbreak homesickness for him.

He has, of course, changed. Innocence is gone. Likewise, his exuberance is much tempered—or else he'd get into trouble much more than he does. He is cautious now. And I am altogether helpless to protect him. No more. I cannot attack the attackers any more.

The sense of general fairness and universal beauty in this world has been compromised for both of us. Various sorts of worldly authorities accomplished that destruction.

Matthew departs this home of his parents for a difficult life, my dear one does. I hugged him. I hugged him very hard, but I could not hug him long, as once among the flowers. There are no fields of yellow flowers anymore.

I hugged him and let him go, and he is gone.

And now I console my loneliness in prayer:

O Holy Father of my son, he bears in your forgiveness his veriest strength. Forgiven, he can forgive—and forgiving, he shall survive this world unto eternity. Never let my boy forget this best of lessons. Never.

Amen.

16

Daughtertalk

I wish the fish took my bait as quickly as my daughter takes the ring of the telephone.

One ring and that child has burst from the bathroom, scorched through the kitchen, and snatched the receiver: "Hello, this's Mary."

One ring! Evidently there are no joys Mary will not forego for the phone. Certainly a long, contemplative, comfortable crouch in a little room is no match for a chat.

Mary doesn't like to be alone. My daughter's gregarious by nature and gladdest when gossiping.

Listen: the other night while she was sleeping—in her bedroom, an hour into her slumber, the door being closed where she lay—the telephone rang. Even before that first ring finished, Mary—sleeping still, her pupils as tiny as pinpricks, smiling in dreamy expectation—Mary went floating down the hallway: "I'll get it," she murmured.

I do not lie. I woke her before she embarrassed herself by sleep-talking.

Ah, but over the telephone that girl *never* embarrasses herself. She's a TJ for skill and aplomb, *Telephone Jockey,* liquid language, opinions on any matter, grace under pressure.

When Mary receives the heavy-breathers' call (as she has), she holds her own cheery conversation until *he* hangs up. "Hello? Hello? Hello?" she chirps. "Oh, poor pitiful-little-mute-man, what's the matter? Asthma? Can't you talk? You think maybe I'm nine-one-one?"—and so forth.

She is undisturbed even by the mentally disturbed, as long as her weapon is the telephone. Mary's an expert.

She's tireless, too.

Howcanateenagertalkforhoursandneverrunoutofwords? Or out of breath either?

And are both of them talking at once? I mean, is the father of the daughter at the other end *also* hearing endless, breathless, uninterrupted news reports about nearly nothing at all? Or when does Mary's interlocutor get to speak?

Well, I believe these children have perfected a method of talk/listening whereby they do both at once with equal energy. I think there's a detachment within the head of the mouth from the ear. Just as, when teens do homework while watching TV, there's an obvious detachment between brain and face. It's an evolutionary phenomenon.

Progress.

Moreover, with the talk/listening method it is possible to attend to five, ten, twenty topics all at the same time. This is why teenagers can discuss seventeen significant issues while flying through the kitchen and out the back door: unkind teachers, no homework again, friends in life-and-death situations requiring immediate visits, don't wait up, and good-bye. While the poor parent, pop-eyed, is still emerging from the consolations of the bathroom and wondering if he heard the telephone ring.

Now, then, the posture for telephone calls will vary according to the caller and the urgency of the call.

They are as follows, depending on who's at the other end:

Girlfriends: Lie on the floor, feet propped on the walls, hair in disarray. Gesture with the free arm. No matter the clothing, no matter the lighting. This is the posture for gossip.

Girlfriends, pastime: Watch TV with the girlfriend on the line—two phones, two TV sets, two running sets of opinions, two bloody shrieks for brothers who, mistaking a phone call for a phone call, switch channels. Also, while watching TV and talk/listening, do one's nails—and blow on them too.

Girlfriends, serious: Sit up, hunch over, hang the hair around one's head as if in private, but speak dramatically, even explosively—especially if discussing some personal insult.

Boyfriends: Laugh a lot. Stand up. Prance, swinging the free arm wildly. Good lighting for glancing in mirrors.

Boyfriends, serious: Sit in a chair. Doodle with pencil or the forefinger. Button all buttons as if dressing well. Low light is preferable. Music too—but not MTV.

Boyfriends, very serious: Absolutely no one else in the room. If a parent should skirt too close to this lair, a hissing will indicate his danger.

Boyfriends, very, very serious: Perfect silence. Weeping.

This last posture the father will notice. He will wait until the call is concluded, and then he will offer his daughter a hug. She has run out of words. No TJ now, no longer tireless, no expert at anything—she is desolated. Her father holds her very tight and hates the phone right now. He hates anyone and any thing that hurts his daughter.

On the other hand, there is no punishment worse than being grounded with telephone silence.

Ask Mary.

For it is on the phone that she renews her spirit again, laughing. Oh, this child laughs at the fleetingest joke and, having started, cannot stop. Tinkling laughter runs into boisterous laughter swells into mighty Mississippis of laughter, till my Mary is left gasping and streaming tears over some fool thing one of them said, which is, of course, not funny in the retelling but which, in fact, is friendship anyway. Plain friendship. Whole and healthy, holy friendship.

And in such moments I love the telephone very much. I appreciate anything that makes my baby lovely again.

But I wonder, as I pass the poor kid squealing on the floor: are these two friends just moaning in one another's ear, saying nothing, yowling like animals? No words? No worthy communication on this expensive and advanced device, but inarticulate giggles and woofings as if they never learned language at all?

Is this what the phone has returned us to, the primitive grunt and the Mary-onic burble?

Actually, no: it's not the invention, it's the daughter. She'll do it off satellites and halfway round the globe; or else by wire; or face-to-face, if she has to. She'll do it cheap or dear—all's one with her. She *must talk,* whether in words her parents recognize or in noises more expressive of the subtler teenage spirit, burps and barks and purrings.

However complex, however progressive technology may get, it is the daughter that does not change. For which pertinacity, saith this father (from within a small, locked, porcelain room, his only throne in a house inhabited by a Princess): *Praise the Lord after all.*

17

The Altar of Motherhood

Deliberate, devout, and beautiful, the woman walks to the altar and places there her precious gift and watches while it is consumed—

How long has this been going on? For eons.

How many people have done it? Myriads. But mostly women.

Then why haven't we been astounded by such holiness? Well, I think we are by nature blind to sacrifice. Even the receivers of this outrageous love don't truly know its depth if they have never felt the wound of it, have felt the sweet blessing only. Perhaps we have to suffer sacrifice in order to understand it.

Perhaps that's why I didn't know my mother well. I mean: I didn't know the quality of her love until I myself experienced her circumstance and did myself make a mother's choices—

Children, honor that woman who for your sake placed on the altar of motherhood some core part of her precious self. Honor and do not neglect her!

In 1985 Thanne and I switched household duties. She went to work full-time, and because mine was the more mobile work, I brought it home. Writing had become my primary profession. Now housekeeping became my primary obsession. From that year forth I took over the cooking, the shopping, the kitchen, the bed, and the bedroom—yea, and the children.

Through the winter and spring of 1985 things went swimmingly. By eight in the morning I was alone in the house, busy in the kitchen, to be sure, but at the same time thinking through the day's writing ahead of me. By nine, dinner was in a crock and I was at the typewriter. For six solid hours thereafter, the writer wrote.

At three in the afternoon the children came home. So writing was done. The writer turned into a father, and the father emerged from his study ready to usher his children everywhere. I cheered their games, I refereed their arguments, I disciplined and pitied and talked and cooked and set the table and timed our dinner to begin at six, when Thanne got home.

Thus the noonday writer and the afternoon father thrived, both of them—so long as they stayed separate.

But then came June. And my dear children came home to stay.

Now, I had committed myself to completing a book-length manuscript that summer, but I trusted my ability to organize and I intended to accomplish the same amount of work now as I had when school was in session. I established a schedule to occupy the kids (with an equal mix of chores and recreation) while I wrote. Of course I would write. There never was a question about such a thing. I was a writer. That was my core *self,* my purpose for being.

But the telephone was suddenly seized with a thousand

fits of ringing a day. And the children ate meals whenever the mood took them. And friends came over, shouting, fighting, laughing, interrupting the sweet symmetry of my schedule (chores and recreation). Okay, so I had to stop writing, come out of my study, put limits on the use of the phone, dismiss kids who were not my own, remind my own (over and over) to clean the kitchen after their meals, and stab my finger for emphasis at the schedule on the refrigerator: "Do, do, *do,* you fools!"

Back to writing again. Whew.

Ah, but even when I didn't rush out of the study, every time a kid raised his voice I had to stop. To listen. To figure out what was going on. Or any time the kids lowered their voices, I had to stop. To listen even harder. Silence is dangerous. And if you can't hear it, you have to go *see* it. So up and out I went after all.

And you cannot schedule arguments. And you can't plan tragedies. So? So I stopped writing. I burst out of my room. I yelled. I arbitrated. I held my poor daughter till she stopped crying. Ach, I stopped, and I stopped! I brought kids here, I drove them there, I answered their questions, I filled out their forms, I took them swimming, and I blew up:

"LEMME ALONE! JUST LET ME ALONE! I'VE GOT TO WRITE!"

("Shhh, Daddy's going crazy.")

Okay, so I stopped writing altogether. That is, I decided it was time for a whole new start, for all of us. I took a week's break from writing, calmed my spirit, jettisoned all that I had (so miserably) written during the first days of summer, quietly instructed the children in the necessities of my job ("It feeds you, sucker!"), and sat down to start all over again, refreshed—because, of course, I *would* start over again. I would surely write. It's who I am, you see—

Can anyone explain to me? Why, if you have told your children never to interrupt you, do they interrupt you with little whispers as if whispering were better? As if whispering proves them obedient after all? I HATE WHISPERING! IT DRIVES WRITER-DADDIES MAD!

Okay, so then why *don't* children interrupt you when they're about to take off for parts of the city you've never yourself had the temerity or the stupidity to enter? And why must the writer-daddy come out of his study to find the house as dead as marble? Wondering where his children have gone? And whether his previous rage is the cause of their present danger? Dumb, dumb, dumb, Daddy!

Three times that summer I stopped, cooled, smiled, gathered my forces, and started all over again. Three times my children slew the book in me. Three times!

But these kids were not bad kids. No, they were just plain kids who needed a parent. It's the order of things. They needed a presence. A mother. But I am so slow to learn. And finally, only experience itself teaches me. By bending me to the right will, the holy way.

Finally, I bowed my head before my children's natural need. Finally, I confessed in my soul, *This is right. These children of mine must take precedence—because they are children and they are mine and they come first—yea, though it consume me—*

Then, then I discovered my mother's mothering and the astonishing quality of her love. Then: when I chose. When I sacrificed the writer-self and consciously renounced my book and offered my children, completely, a parent. I had to do the former to allow the latter. These were the same act after all. I had to let the core of me die—for a while, at least—that they might properly live.

Ah, Mother, every summer since then I have thought of you and of all your sisters through the ages. I see you, darling, distinctly—as in a vision. I see deep, and I see this: that once there lay in the precinct of many mothers' souls some precious personal thing. Some talent, some private dream. The characteristic by which they defined their *selves* and their purpose for being. To write? Maybe. To run a marathon? Or to run a company? Yes. Yes.

But then the baby came home, and then you and others like you made a terrible, terribly lovely choice. You reached into your soul and withdrew that precious thing and lifted it up before your breast and began to walk. Deliberate and utterly beautiful, you strode to an altar of love for this child and placed there the talent, the dream, some core part of your particular *self*—and in order to mother another, you released it. There came for you a moment of conscious, sacred sacrifice. In that moment the self of yourself became a smoke, and the smoke went up to heaven as perpetual prayer for the sake of your children.

And when it was voluntary, it was no less than divine. Never, never let anyone force such a gift from any woman!— for then it is not sacrifice at all. It is oppression.

But never, either, dear children, take such an extraordinary love for granted. It is holy. For this, in the face of such women, is the mind of Christ, who emptied himself for us. And then again, for us.

Ah, Mother, I am so slow to know, but now I know—and out of the knowledge wherewith my own children have burdened me I thank you. From an overflowing heart, I thank you, Mother, for your motherhood.

18

Commencement

Outside my study window, just this side of Bayard Park, sit two boys on the hood of a cream Camaro—in the process of becoming men.

How old are they? Well, their backs are to me. I see an occasional profile: sweet, smooth cheeks on the one boy, an innocent twinkle in his eye, rather chubby. The other is leaner, with broad, capable shoulders and a low brow. Athletic, obviously. God has given him a quality body. But how old? Seventeen? Eighteen at the most. Boys.

But they're speeding toward manhood with grave purpose.

And I grieve at the process. I am sick at heart for the men they wish to become and the means whereby they intend to achieve it.

Jekyll drank something, and Hyde sprang forth. These, too, begin by drinking—although their ritual is much more elaborate and clearly rehearsed. It smacks of tradition. It's been handed down to them. And watch! In thirty minutes they shall be men. Men after the image of . . . someone. There is some model in their minds according to which they are shaping themselves.

Men.

Okay, so lean child hands chubby child a pint, the flat bottle shrewdly concealed in brown paper. They exchange a bolder bottle of orange juice. They suck. They stare across the park, unspeaking yet. They are thinking great thoughts, obviously. They are, at this point, discovering that they have as much right to think great thoughts as any president of the United States, and the capacity, too. Or else they are merely waiting for the warm transformation of their minds so that the great thoughts already thought, already lodged above, might be released and descend. They suck. A car drives by. The bottles slide down between their thighs, but neither child ceases his stare. This is a solemn moment. They suck.

A little conversation now begins between them. I can't hear it; but by the nodding and the pursing of lips, I know: they consider their words to be uttered in wisdom; and they are in agreement together, lean kid and large kid. The great thoughts are coming down, now, like a sober rain. Manhood is arising. It is not just that they are beginning to feel good, but that they are feeling good *about themselves,* in every respect children of this progressive world. Aye, the smiling world should be proud of two who learn so well. Moreover, each of these feels he's in fine company.

It's time for the second agent of their maturation.

While lean fellow stretches his marvelous spine, hunches his athletic shoulders, and rolls his neck (gazing forever across the park), chunky fellow produces a Ziploc plastic bag. The shreds of dried vegetation inside are most carefully shaken onto white paper, the which is balanced on a finger, licked, rolled, and twisted at the ends. Sealed. Skillfully shapen and sealed. I am impressed by the earnest attention to ceremony given this act. There's more than mere practicality in chubby child's gestures; there is symbol and meaning and obedience, as if he were priesting at an altar and handling sacred elements. There is, clearly, a "right way" to roll a roach. And he who does it "right" is an initiate. He's passed some test. He is a man.

The white twist, now, is lit with fire. It burns. The round cheese-chunk of a fellow sucks on it. Then, with sacramental care—not looking at his brother, keeping his own face passive, gazing across the park—he passes it to the bean beside him, who performs the same rite: sucking. They are sharing

Conversation develops a new weight. It becomes louder.

Lean kid slips from the hood of the Camaro. He begins to wave his arms, to stab the air with a pointed forefinger, to snap his head back at particularly critical strokes of rhetoric.

Lean kid is preaching.

Great thoughts, thoughts first conceived in an alcoholic fume then passed from mind to mind in devout conversation, thoughts consecrated by Mary Jane's numb benediction, these thoughts have now become *opinions*. Lean boy has opinions. He has, by the flash of his eye and the crack of his delivery, judgments to pass on many things within the world. Clearly, he feels he has a calling and the right to make them. Even so, he is above the world he criticizes. Even so, he has arrived. He is a man.

See him strut and frown? He's a passionate fellow. Do you see him beat his chest? Lo: *he* is the sweeter substance of all his thought. He has elevated *himself* by the elevation of his mind. There is no doubt, now: he can do great deeds. And do you see how he receives the approval of his brother, who roars and thumps the hood of the Camaro? He is not only wise, he is right! Hear him shout, despite the glances of more conventional passersby. Not only right: yo!—he is free.

Lean baby and chubby baby, they are men now. They possess a certain swelling self-importance. They've found their places in the universe.

And I grieve.

Where are the other men, the men who served as models for this travesty? Where are the true adults—by years, adults—who considered their lifestyles to be their "own business" and did not notice younger, watchful, malleable eyes desiring to make it *their* business, too? Where are these heroes and teachers of the children, these failures in plain responsibility, these liars of the good life, these fathers, older brothers, uncles, friends? Frauds! Around their necks should be hung the millstone Jesus described. Carve in that millstone the epitaph, *Just doin' my own thing. Ain't hurtin' no one.* Then cast them into the depths of the sea for having tempted little ones to sin.

Little children, strutting men!

God help them all.

In the end these two step away from their Camaro and perform a final rite of virility. They reverence the tree.

Lean fool and chubby fool stand side by side in silence, facing the trunk of a huge oak, their legs spread, their hands hidden below, their heads bowed down, peeing.

Then they zip. And then they drive the Camaro away to confront their destiny somewhere in the humdrum traffic.

19

P.U.T.T.T.

I don't want cereal on my kitchen floor. Does anyone? Is there anywhere a rational person who is not distressed by cereal on the kitchen floor?

Well, it grinds the no-wax floor I've just no-waxed. It murders the shine and my good mood. At night it hectors my sleep with dreams of a house buried in Cheerios. In the morning it sticks to my socks. It blackens dried dribbles of orange juice.

So what? So am I a lunatic to ask my children not to spill cereal on the kitchen floor? Is this a law too difficult to bear? No, this is basic and reasonable cleanliness.

It's unarguably healthy.

Then why, when hopping on one foot and declaring myself unhappy about cereal on the kitchen floor, do my children gape at me as if I'm countermanding some previous command that they *should* spill cereal on the floor, together with milk and a little orange juice? Why do they indicate my insanity then? And why do their wounded eyes call me the only warden in the world upset by a little cereal?

O fathers and mothers of the world, unite!

And what about homework? Does my daughter do her homework to benefit *me*? Am I enlightened by her learning? Will my name appear on the report card? Will I get a job thereby? Well, of course not. I am myself not a whit improved by her endeavor.

But then why, when I require of her the work that shall reward none but her, does she groan? Why does she pout and glower at me as if I've just ruined her life for my own satisfaction? I HATE GLOWERING!

Why do my children, in the best of moods, humor me— and, in the worst, act punished, imprisoned, unjustly troubled by a mindless giant?

Yours too?

O parents, unite!

My second son, whose back ripples with quick strength on a basketball court, is suddenly crippled by the mere mention of the lawn mower. It is his job to walk the dog. He has never walked a dog in his life, poor troubled soul.

And I have considered the regular series of emotions that cripple *me* when that same son is late for his curfew:

1. Mild annoyance (the kid is snitching minutes, though he promised to be home on time);

2. Anger, hotter by the hour;

3. Earnest worry, laced with guilt (is he hurt?—why did I blame the innocent child?);

4. And finally, crashing rage at his return and the explanation he offers, words meant to calm me by their reasoned and weighty consideration: "Uh, I forgot."

Every night, Matthew?

And can anyone explain to my own mother's son how it is that the lack of clean clothes is my fault?—when the cracker-jack kid neglected to throw her dirty clothes into the laundry?

Is it written somewhere that children must dress slowly,

making everyone late for important occasions? Late and angry? I HATE TO BE LATE!

And who said that my cologne (and my socks and my razor and my room and my car and my wife's whole wardrobe) is theirs just because they inhabit the same house with us?

And did you know that TV is a teenager's constitutional right? Actually, noise is the right—any sort of noise: booming, strumming, shrieking, giggling.

And did you know that teenagers regularly detonate clothes-bombs in their bedrooms? The quicker the mess, the gladder the kid.

What do they do with our money anyway? Eat it?

O parents, one and all, what manner of thing have we sheltered all these years? What have we taken to our soft bosoms, which sprouted thereafter a vulture's beak and a taste for the flesh of progenitors? Teenagers! A breed apart.

It's a relatively new creature, this teen. For most of the world's history teenagers didn't exist. Until the last few hundred years, children ceased dependence upon their parents at fourteen, fifteen, sixteen, then shouldered their own apprenticeships, their labors and land and families. That wasn't considered too tender an age then; it certainly is no tender age today, but rough-cut and ready and stronger than I!

Parents, I have two proposals to make:

1. That once again we abolish teenagerhood; offer our fourteen-year-olds all rights of maturity, all the freedoms, and therewith all the responsibilities as well; throw them a *true* come-out party and give them luggage as a gift and mean it. If such a ritual of transition is universally observed, it'll benefit the nation whole. Think how much energy would be converted to solid work and taxable income—the which is now spent in malls on walking, talking, preening only. Think how we might augment the military, allay the national debt, and regain our place as first among industrial countries. Think of one father who will sleep unhectored by dreams of cereal on his kitchen floor.

Or, if my first proposal proves impossible, consider my second:

2. P.U.T.T.T. An organization entitled *Parents United To Tolerate Teenagers.*

Teenagerhood is, in fact, the kid's leave-taking from the family—extended over a longer period than in generations before. It is a normal process after all—a time when she learns independence and practices it, even while she is yet physically dependent upon her parents; a time of strife, then, and of inherent contradiction, but not of anything sick or sinful or wrong. The tension between independence and dependence causes violent shifts in attitudes. It confuses parent and child alike. The rules of relationship change daily; so what is a parent to *be* from Sunday to Tuesday?—A companion? A confidant? A cop? A teacher? Zoo keeper? Cheerleader? God?

Precisely during this period, dear parents, unite.

The process of separation is good and necessary, already defined in Genesis chapter two: *Therefore shall a man LEAVE his father and his mother, and shall CLEAVE unto his wife: and they shall be one flesh.* For any proper cleaving hereafter, there must be a true leaving now. The irritation, then, the pain of separation, the emotion and the provocation, the trouble and the break itself cannot be abolished, and it should not be avoided. It will be. Teens will bug us. And we them.

But we, their parents, might regularly support one another. Let's find stability with those who have managed (or who are managing) similar challenges, rather than demanding stability from the teens who, by the nature of their present passage, are as unstable as water. They simply cannot give it now.

Parents, let us laugh together by telling tales of the idiocy of these tall children. Laughter diminishes problems by granting a blessed release and a realistic perspective. Let's talk seriously, too; exchange advice; discover how very common, after all, is all that we thought bedeviled our family alone. And let's pray out loud. For each child by name. And for the parents. Because God is God of teenagers too. God is the one parent who shall *not* be superseded. And God will work internally in the confusing kid, using ways we can't even see.

For now we must love at a distance; but God never departs the intimate heart of the child. Never.

Ah, parents, attend to your own consolations now when the job of parenting *is* a job, an assignment, not a pleasure—and you will become a consolation for the teen who is as bewildered as yourself.

20

To the Pools of Siloam

*I*t's been two seasons now since I saw her, but because of the tremendous respect she inspired in me (and then, as well, the pity) I can't forget her.

It picks at the back of my mind, over and over again, asking: *What does she remind me of?*

Something remarkable.

Last spring a duck entered our backyard journeying eastward, eleven little ducklings in file behind her. It was an outrageous appearing, really, since we live in the midst of the concrete city. The only waters east of us are the pools at the state hospital, four miles away, which distance is an odyssey! Between here and there are vast tracts of humanity, fences, houses, shopping malls—and immediately to our east, Bayard Park of tall trees and lawns.

Yet this duck moved her brood with a quick skill as if she knew exactly where she was going.

Buff brown generally, vague markings on her wings, a smooth pate with a cowlick at the back, she and her name were the same: blunt and unremarkable. The ducklings were puffballs with butch haircuts, obedient and happy. Big-footed, web-footed, monstrous-footed, floppy-footed, the children followed their mother as fast as drips down windowpanes, peeping, questioning, keeping together, trusting her judgment.

And she, both blunt and busy, led them into our yard, which is surrounded by a wooden palisade fence. Maybe she came this way for a rest.

But we have a dog. He rose to his feet at the astonishing sight. He raised his ears and woofed. The duck backpedaled to the wall of the house and turned eastward under the eaves' protection and waddled hard, her ducklings in mad zip behind her. But the dog is leashed and could not reach the wall. This part of the passage, at least, was safe. The next was not.

Without pausing, the buff duck spread her wings, beat the air, and barely cleared the fence, landing in the middle of Bedford Avenue between our yard and the park. There she set up a loud quacking, like a reedy woodwind: *Come! Come!*

Eleven ducklings scurried to the fence, then raced along it till they found a crack: *Plip! Plip!*—they popped through as quick as they could, but their mother must have been driven into the park. By the time they gained the wider world she had disappeared. The babies bunched in confusion, peeping, peeping grievously. One bold soul ventured down Bedford to the alley behind our yard. The others returned through the fence.

Immediately the mother was back on Bedford, the one bold child behind her, scolding the rest like an angry clarinet: *Now! Here! Come here now!*

Well, in a grateful panic ten ducklings rushed the crack in the fence, thickening there, pushing, burning with urgency, trying hard to obey their mother—

Not fast enough.

A car roared south on Bedford. Another. The duck beat retreat to the farther curb. Joggers came jogging. A knot of teenagers noticed the pretty flow of ducklings from under our fence and ran toward it. The tiny flock exploded in several directions. The mother's cries grew hectic and terrified: *Come! Come!*—her beak locked open. She raced up and down the park's edge, and there was but the one puffball following her.

The simple unity of twelve was torn apart. My city is deadly to certain kinds of families.

Five ducklings shot back and forth inside our yard now, but the hole through the fence led to roaring horrors and they couldn't persuade themselves to hazard it again though they could hear their mother. That unremarkable duck (no!—intrepid now and most remarkable) was hurling herself in three directions, trying to compose her family in unity again: eastward she flew into the park, south toward violent alleys, then back west to the impassive fence. *Hear me now, hear me and come!* Her children were scattered. She was but one.

I saw a teenager chase one duckling. He was laughing gaily in the game. He reached down and scooped up the tiny life in his great hand and peered at it and then threw it up into the air. The baby fell crazily to the ground. The youth chased it again.

"Don't!" I yelled.

"Why not?" the kid said, straightening himself. "What? Does this duck belong to you?"

But where was the mother now? I didn't see her anywhere. And now it was bending into the later afternoon.

I poured some water into a pan and placed it by the back wall of the house for those ducklings still dithering within our yard. They huddled away from the dog. But the dog had lost interest. They crept sometimes toward the hole in the fence. Now and again a duckling looked through. Their peeping, peeping was miserable. What do you do for innocents in the city—both the wild and the child? By nightfall they had all vanished.

No, not all. I can tell you of two.

The next day we heard a scratching in the vent pipe of our

clothes dryer. I went down in the basement and disconnected the shaft and found a shivering duckling who must have fallen down from the outside opening. Perhaps it had sought cover and didn't know the cave went down so deep. It had spent a long dark night alone in its prison.

And then at church on Sunday a friend of mine said, "Weirdest thing! I saw this duck crossing highway 41—"

"What?" I cried. "A duck? Alone?"

"Well, no, not alone," said my friend. "I almost ran over her. I guess she didn't fly on account of baby ducks can't fly, and she was protecting it."

"Michelle," I said, "what do you mean *it*? How many ducklings did she have?"

"One. Just one."

There have passed two seasons, I say, since I encountered this blunt, buff duck—and still in my heart I whisper as I did then, *Godspeed* with honor and pity. *Godspeed, remarkable creature, tenacious and loving.*

And now I know what she reminds me of.

Of single-parent families in a largely indifferent world.

She reminds me of that impoverished mother (Oh, my culpable country!) who has small means to nourish and raise and protect her children. I have met that mother far too often with far too little to offer her. Mighty is her love. Illogical, absurd, and marvelous is her love for the children. And terrible is her sorrow for the loss of any one of them. The world may not enlarge her love or else diminish her sorrow. The world may in fact begrudge whatever little thing it gives her. Worse: the world can be dangerous to the family whole and to her children in particular.

But she loves. This mother knows from the beginning that the children will be chased, harassed, scorned, beaten, belittled—both by raggedy folks and by the upright and civil people of her city. She knows that one child may tumble down black shafts of a blatant disregard and another into drugs and another into crime and another into despair. From the beginning their prospects must wring her heart with a tight anxiety. She labors to give them a life for a while and some esteem and safety—and against desperate odds, marvelously, she loves.

To this one I say, *Godspeed, good parent, all the way east to the pools of Siloam and your children's maturity.*

And to the holy community of the church I say: *Help her! Surround this single parent, mother or father, with love and a service equal to her own. No: with a love equal to God's, whom you are sent to represent!*

In God's name, help her.

21

To Mary, at Her Confirmation

*D*ear Mary:

God loved you first. Please, child, remember that.

Before Mom and I fell in love with you (and we were two of the first to fall in love with you) God loved you.

Before we even met your chunky self or knew what sort of kid was living behind those gazing-blue, hungry-blue, those curious, sky-laughing-blue eyes; before you grabbed my finger the first time; before you came somewhat shocked and blood-streaked into the air of this world; before you bulked in Mom's womb, lying in the cradle of her pelvis; before you wriggled secretly in the deepest regions of the woman's being, when none on earth was aware that you existed—in that dark, solitary time, that holy and unknown moment when you had scarcely come to be, when you had no name, no human shape, no thought, no dreams nor fears nor fancies; when, like the primal cell, you had but being only and all the rest of you was possibility—then, Mary, *even then* God loved you!

Yes, yes, I know: it's impossible for anyone to remember that far back. But that's precisely the point: God remembers. God loved the dot that was you and contemplated the woman you would become. He it was who formed your inward parts, who knit you together in your mother's womb. Your frame was not hidden from him when you were being made in secret, intricately wrought in the depths of the earth.

I tell you all this, Mary, in order to prepare you for the difficulty hidden in the happy day to come this Sunday.

This Sunday is the day of your confirmation.

On your own two legs, in your own voice, independently and publicly and according to your own sole faith, you will declare that Jesus is your Lord and Savior. I won't say it for you this time, nor with you, nor to you. You, child, will confess it all alone.

You will say, "I believe. This is who I am now: I believe in Jesus Christ, God's only Son, born of the Virgin Mary, who suffered and was crucified and died and was buried and on the third day rose from the dead. All this *for me!* It is my life. It is my soul and my self."

You will say that, and I will listen, and I will marvel that my child has grown up—both in the world and in the faith; and I will recognize, dear Mary, that my child has also grown away from me.

Oh, yes. One's faith is more crucial to one's continued existence than one's profession. This particular decision requires infinitely more maturity than the decision made in a ballot booth, than the decision to fight in the military, than any decision the world calls "mature." When, therefore, you make it, girl, you will have become independent. You'll be in spirit an adult and a child no longer. Your believing will need me less and less as more and more you turn your face directly to God. My fatherhood decreases. You, kid—you shall be free of me.

Listen: crack that cocoon! I praise the chrysalid change in

thee. I want it for you. You must grow. It is good and necessary.

And you yourself have been yearning for such independence many and many a year now. Here it is.

Mary.

It is in your nature to fly!

But right there is the difficulty hidden in the event.

For one day in your free flight you will look down and see how high you've gone and discover how lonely you are and how dangerous the world is—and you will be afraid.

As delicious as it may seem, independence is a terrible thing.

In that day you will cry out for me, and I won't be there as I have been there before—no, not in the same way. I won't be able to answer as I have. Because you shall have left me. So maybe your loneliness will be sharpened by the silences. Maybe it will pierce to the soul. *Daddy!* you'll cry. *I'm falling! I'm falling*—And the fact that I do not come and hug you as I have in the past (as I will yet tomorrow in your high delight and tension) will seem to you monstrous.

O Mary! Dear Mary, *then* remember that God loved you first. God always loved you and will sustain you always.

My love had a beginning. It is time-struck. Mine is a human love, child—and though I will love you to the end, and though I will want with all my heart to catch you when you fall, I can't. I can't. As you grow up, I grow weak. I simply cannot parent you forever. To me you are not forever a child.

But to the God who never dies you, Mary Wangerin, will be a child forever and ever.

Therefore, though it may be terrifying when you cry out and I do not answer, it won't finally be disastrous. It will throw you upon the strength of an abiding, unchanging, merciful God, the same One whom you will confess on Sunday. In the day of your terrible fall, that confession shall find its perfect fulfillment and you your first Father.

He whose love was earlier than mine will persist past mine forever.

I have a photograph of you, my Mary. You are sitting, reading a book. Your head is bent. Your shining blonde hair hangs down on one side. You are soft in a striped, flannel nightgown, and you are deep in meditations. It is as though your spirit has already flown out of you—into the tale you're reading. You are beautiful and you are gone, both at once.

When I look at that photograph, my heart hurts a bit.

I think, *Where has the girl gone? So far, so far away: what world does she now inhabit, whereto I cannot follow her?*

That single picture instructs me of the future when you shall fly. I ache against the future.

But then I, too, take an infinite comfort in this: that God loved you first. I may be earthbound, but the Spirit of God flies farther and faster than even my lightsome daughter flies. So I shall say, in my own loneliness hereafter, *But she is not alone.*

For wither shalt thou go, my Mary, from the Spirit of the Lord? If you mount to the heavens (and you may, upon the feather of some fantasy) God is there. If you make your bed in the pit of the dead (and you may, in natural sympathy with them that suffer), God is there. If you take the wings of the morning and dwell in the uttermost parts of the sea, even there God's hand shall lead thee, and his right hand shall cover thee.

It is your confession. It is my comfort.

I give you, my child, to God.

When you sturdily confirm the covenant you have with the mighty Deity in sweet Jesus Christ, then you leave me. Then I let you go. The gestures shall be mutual, and so they shall be good.

But they would not be possible or good if you left your heavenly Father, or if he let you go. But you do not leave him now for your high flight. No, no, the good Lord spreads his own broad wings to soar with you wherever you go. *He* shall bear you forth in the morning on eagles' wings, and in the evening *he* shall cover you with his pinions, and I shall be content to grow old in the knowledge, *She is not alone. He who loved her first shall love her always. Amen.*

22

County Fair:
A Fiction the Father
Remembers

*H*ey-a! Hey-a! Pick yo col-ah!"

The young man has a wire collar round his neck and, fixed to that, a microphone. His hands are free. He prowls inside a rectangular booth in electric light, eyeing the crowd that wanders by. The night is thick with humidity.

"Hey-a! Hey-a!" He's a sawdust barker. His is just one of a hundred games of chance at a county fair in southern Indiana.

"Hey-a! The mouse in a hole, an' ev'ry won's a winnah!"

There are tight rows of makeshift tents beneath oak trees, tables walled on two sides, the winding lanes of tired carny barkers, corn dogs, tawdry contests, prizes that smell of lipstick and motor oil. Hey, pop a balloon. Hey, knock the bottles over, shoot electric shots, pick a duck, flip a dime. Ev'ry won's a winnah.

And this man's booth is open on all four sides, four counters with vertical stripes of various colors. Put your money on a color. In the booth is a glass-enclosed turntable that radiates the same bright colors from its center, like the vanes of a windmill. Holes form a wide circle around the edge of the table, one hole in the top of every vane of color. A white box sits dead in the middle of all, and tinier holes freckle it with a smiley-face.

"Hey-a!" the young man shouts. He's eyeing a couple now floating out of the night in his direction. "The mouse in a hole, and a doll for the dolly," he says. Both the boy and the girl approaching wear tight jeans. They amble each with a hand in the other's hip pocket. "Get the girl a gift," the barker commands without conviction. "Demonstrate ya manhood." The lad looks up. He has lank hair that hangs in clumps like horse's bells. When he grins his face slopes south. He grins. The lass has a sharp jaw, sharp nose, sharp, etched eyebrows. At her age this face presents a certain fierce delicacy, like veined china. But at twenty-four she will look hard and old. Backwoods.

The girl bites her lip and gooses her boyfriend—sly, with a flash in her eye. At the moment she is dominant.

"Do it, Ray," she says.

Ray does it.

So the barker has a quarter on the color green.

And now three blonde girls weave through the crowd and rush like popping chickadees to the counter and slap down three quarters, giggling, all on blue. They must have made a common decision. Each blonde head is a tangle of exactly the same hair. Each pretty shoulder has the same white nylon jacket. Every little ear is pierced several times over; pearly tics march up the earlobes. All three mouths mush gum. The little maids are flush with friendship, and it's late, but who's to tell them it's time to be home?

The blonde girls jostle each other, disjoining their hips in hammer-throws left and right.

"Well, he didn't ack-shully *see me,* y'know."

"You said the boy'ud faint at the sight of you."

"He does! He gawks! He passes notes in school."

"You said he'd faint."

"Mister, spin the wheel. Let yer mouse out. What're we waiting for?" Four quarters on the counter, he's waiting for more.

"Hey-a, hey-a," he mourns into his microphone, glancing at the flow of people.

"Mister!"

If the barker were older, he'd be wearing a buttoned short-sleeve shirt, stretched at the belly, loose at the back. If he were anyone else he'd be wearing worn dress shoes. In fact, he's very young, whippet-thin, and sad. He wears a white T-shirt and the sort of work boots one takes into the fields or else mucks the barn out in. In fact, he's the son of a South Dakota farmer. It's nearly midnight. He is exhausted.

"Mister! What're we waiting . . . yow! Look at *you!*"

Suddenly an enormous man materializes from the slow river of people passing. Bandy-legged, glacial white and mountainous, mostly hairless, this man's eyes are small and moist, his lips both full and moist. By the diffusion of his piggy eyes one would suppose a sleepy rage in him. Or liquor. Or imbecility. His wrists are creased like a baby's. His fingers are stubby.

"Well?" the barker speaks into the mike. "You gonna watch, you gonna play?"

The huge man squints, stands still a long minute, then gouges his pocket and claps down upon the color red . . . a nickel.

Ray's girlfriend jumps at the sound. Skittish person. Ray himself looks but says nothing. The barker sighs. "It's a quarter," he says.

The moon-bald man raises a fat hand and covers his eyes as if he's thinking. Then he slams the hand flat on the coin. Red. Evidently, it's not a quarter. It's a nickel.

In spite of herself, Ray's girlfriend jumps again and then grows angry at herself.

"Hey!" chirp the blonde triplets. "Hey, mister, you gonna let this chump get away with that?"

The barker sighs.

The chump stands stolid, mild, immovable.

"Ray?" whispers his girlfriend, keeping her face down but plucking at his elbow. "Ray?"

"Mister," the three children protest, "he put a nickel down. That's only a nickel."

The barker rubs his stomach as if in an increasing pain, but he says nothing.

"Ray?"

"Well, trick you!" In concert the three blonde girls snatch their quarters from blue and flit into the night like sparrows. "Cheat! Cheat!" they cry.

"Ray?"

"What!" snaps Ray of the languid hair, still staring down at the colors. He yanks his elbow back to himself.

The girlfriend shrinks, measuring distance between the boy on one side and the huge bland man on the other, touching neither. "Nothin'," she says.

Ray's face is taut with concentration, thinking, thinking, working the muscles.

For the second time the enormous man slaps the color red as if to say, *You gonna play?*—though in fact he says nothing. He makes a low moan. He rolls his piggy eyes. His arm bumps the body of the sharp girl, who suddenly jumps and shrieks, "Let's get outta here!"

Well, but Ray doesn't move. Dominance is shifting. With tremendous concentration the lean lad takes the quarter from the counter, drops it in his pocket, pulls out a coin purse, and from that picks a nickel. Ray puts a nickel on green, then folds his arms across and waits. Manhood has spoken.

The barker sighs.

He is working the mouse game because the farm went into receivership. It simply drowned in the drought of several summers. And then his father, a Lutheran of Teutonic silences, attempted suicide. Neither father nor mother nor son talked once about the attempt or cried together. They worked the scrabble earth as if it truly produced. They worked as if they did not have to lose it. And then, in the silence of a dark morning, the son left. He intended his absence to relieve his parents of responsibility. Whether it did or not, he doesn't know. He considered his departure a way of loving them. He doesn't know.

So he sighs, and he doesn't argue. He cranks the handle that turns the table and opens the box that frees the mouse. The mouse creeps out and crouches in electric light, rotating on an earth of table. Everyone watches. Every won's a winnah. The mouse darts toward the edge of the table and pops down a hole. Green.

No one is smiling. The game is over.

The barker reaches up and hoists a teddy bear from its hook and hands it to the winnah, the lad of the lank hair.

But before the boy can take it, the tiny-eyed giant explodes, whirls, smashes the bear to the counter, and pins it.

The poor girlfriend jumps again, snapping her teeth together with a click.

"You," says the boy, shuddering, "you, uh, want it?"

But the man sucks his moist lips into his mouth and shakes his head. He takes his nickel. He turns and lumbers away into the night.

So does the boy. So does the girl. Everyone leaves the prize behind. And the young barker is left alone.

He sighs. He reaches under the counter and pulls the plug that cuts the lights. He strips himself of the microphone. He gathers the mouse from its drum and drops it in the white box and sits down on the ground in darkness and bows his head and, for the first time since leaving the farm, he weeps.

23

Calitha Wangia, Go, Go, Go!

*D*ear Talitha:

Mom and I are in the house alone, now. You were the last to leave, kid, and the first to go so far away.

Costa Rica.

Your choice. *You* decided to become a foreign exchange student, *you* initiated the process, *you* chose the country, *you*—bold, brown, and not a ghost of fear in you. Flat, absolute assurance. A mouth-smacking, hip-popping, cocksure swagger. What in high school they call "a attitude," as in: *That girl got a attitude.*

Well, Miss Attitude, I miss you.

Yes, yes, when you were here you wore me out with your thousand ideas, making *my* mind up for me, answering *my* telephone, telling *my* people what *you* thought I wanted, hanging up before I could tell them myself, then telling me what you told them. Huh!

You knew everything for everybody.

Told your mother how to vote, how to drive, what to do with the rest of her life.

Told officers of the law *your* notion of the law.

Made me scared for you, girl. *For* you. This is a dangerous arrogance when others do, in fact, hold authority over you. Ah, but you told the mayor how to run his city. You told the school superintendent how to reward teachers. (I do not lie. You know that what I say is the historical, accurate truth.)

And then you, Talitha Michal Wangerin, told the President of the United States how to run the country.

Yes!

While I was lecturing in Minneapolis during the Gulf War last year, I switched on CNN Headline News, and there you were, sticking your face into the television camera and out my TV screen—a scowl on you as wide as America and fiercer than missiles: "President Bush!" you were saying, even before the announcer had finished her word about opinions from the street. "President Bush!" you were shouting, dressed in the African National Congress colors, red and yellow and green, a pillbox hat and a loose robe to declare your heritage *and* your politics at once thereby.

"PRESIDENT BUSH, WADDAYA MEAN, A NEW WORLD ORDER? IF IT'S A NEW WORLD ORDER, WHAT ABOUT SOUTH AFRICA? WHAT'CHOO GONNA DO 'BOUT THE OLD ORDER DOWN THERE?"

Yow, kid! I couldn't escape your attitude and that crass, know-it-all arrogance even in the frozen north. You hounded me from Atlanta to Minneapolis and beyond—for within the week your quote appeared by virtue of the AP Wire Service in newspapers across the country. Everywhere I went I read you, over and over. My single saving factor was that you had a speech impediment. In order to woo the boys from Kentucky you talked like Kentucky. Black Kentucky. So street and so black the members of our black congregation said, "That girl is practicin' black!" Even the best reporter could not keep up with you, and so your name was printed "Calitha Wangia." At least I would not be tarred with your opinion. President Bush couldn't get through you to me.

Nevertheless, I feared for you, the child who had not the sense to fear for herself. I stretched my spirit nationwide to protect you by my own sheer yearning and by desperate prayer. You wore me out!

Oh, but I miss you, girl.

You have grown so beautiful these last years. And this self-assurance is, I believe, a gift from God. You have the ingredients of a leader.

Costa Rica! Nothing seems too far for you. Nothing seems too high, nothing too difficult, and there is nothing you will not risk, nothing blocked by your size or by your gender—or by your race.

Talitha, I recognize in you a wondrous freedom despite the odds. Where the world erected walls around you, you cut doorways and walked on through.

You're "mixed," as they say. You are the marvelous mixing of white and black bloods. In someone lesser that combination might have shut both the white world and the black world against her, but you have used the double blood for entrance into both.

You're adopted. But that is no impediment. You have, to your mind, twice the parents of lesser children, and before you're done with your investigations you will have found them all. I verily believe this. You will have drawn from all of us every leverage of intelligence and authority and history and skill—and you will have told each of us how to live our lives.

You're female. No restrictions there that you choose to acknowledge. Several times you've decked the male that bothered you—and the boy was decked indeed. Nor have you been persuaded by the traditional notions concerning which professions are open to women; rather, you are seeking your life's work according to your own internal interests.

And if there was any lid on your intellect, you blew it off by perseverance, self-discipline, goal-setting, and goal-achievement. That's how you got to Costa Rica.

And that's wisdom, kid. It's the sort of maturity which *makes* an adult, no matter how young one is—and which, if it is lacking, keeps one a child, no matter how old that one has grown to be.

Daughter, I miss you not only because you've crossed the sea away from me, but also because you've crossed the mountain of maturity: no, you're not a kid anymore. You have departed childhood. My baby girl is gone. She is gone and she shall never come back again.

Mom and I are in the house alone.

We are sad for the loss of children and, too, for the loss of our own parenthood. Ah, but we do at the same time rejoice in the woman that has emerged.

Dear Woman (yes, the same Talitha that wore me out), I worry less for you now, precisely because of that old brass boldness which used to trouble us all. Cockiness hath ripened into genuine confidence. And I myself—I do in confidence, therefore, release you to your womanhood and to the world. *This one will make it,* I whisper. *In spite of the evils which she shall encounter, and the walls thereof, this one shall surely shine.*

I worry less, I say—but I love you no less than before. In fact, I love you more richly, as one adult to another. I love you with honor, now—not just with pity and fear and watchfulness. I love you, lady, with a nearly speechless respect. And my love looks forward to the tremendous significance that you shall *be* hereafter, thou tough young leader.

You could say that I am arrogant about you, that I am mouth-smacking, hip-popping cocksure about this travelin' woman, here at the start of her long life's voyage. You could say I got a attitude:

I am downright proud of you, Talitha.

Godspeed, sweet child.

And you, most wondrously free woman, come home soon.

I miss you.

Dad

24

A Bidding for the Children

*L*ord, it is time: we pray for our children.

—Not only for them in their infancy, when disease or accident alone might harm them;

—Not only for them in childhood, when their dreams begin and school is hard and our own discipline's the hardest thing they must endure;

—Not only for them in adolescence, when their bodies inflame and engorge and grow clumsy and embarrass them; when their peers become their juries, a glaring light in which they flourish or wither, either one or both, daily;

—No, not even especially for them in their adolescence, since the systems surrounding them then are essentially a dry run at adulthood and not yet the real thing; high school, with its academics and athletics, is an excellent mimic of the crasser, unappeasable world to come, but it is only a mimic; there is forgiveness still in high school; that system is still on their side, whether they know it or not, having been organized to benefit them;

—Therefore, though we pray for our children in the confused, confusing period of the teenage years, and though our children feel much in need of a divinity then, it is not *that* time which we most cover in our bidding robes—for still then we parents can do for our children, can physically and financially and wisely help them, can save them from scrapes, can command them toward the right action, can worry them to finish their homework, can shout and plead and hug and smile and comfort to some effect.

No, it is at their entrance into actual adulthood that we pray.

Because at adulthood we are (and we must be) done. We must let go.

To do more than this is to cripple a kid.

But when we let go, what else can we do but pray?

Now when we release our offspring into his and her own care, it is no dry run. The boat's in the ocean, now to sail or else to founder, while we watch helplessly from shore. And there will be sun and easy breezes. But we who watch, who have been adults too long, know that the weather changes. There will be tempests and an absolute requirement of skill, strength, and earnest faith. And does our son have them? And can our daughter hack it now? Oh, Lord! We watch, we watch and pray.

Now our adult offspring must suffer the real consequences of their action.

Carelessness isn't cute any more, a quirk of her endearing personality. Forgetfulness can ruin a credit rating (*Does she know what that means?* says her mother, and her father says, *Hush up. You know it's time to let her handle it alone.*)

Insolence can lose a job. Thoughtlessness can anger dangerous people. Laziness can, literally, initiate the starvation of a young man. (*What is he thinking of? He's going to hurt, and he could avoid it right now!* says his father, and his mother murmurs, *Hush. He's on his own.*)

But arrogance and selfishness and immoderate ambition

and the belief that one has the right to satisfy his own desires can land a fellow in jail. It can break a parent's heart, since everything the child does and every consequence the child causes himself (whether good and honorable or ill and deadly) the parent suffers too, in spirit, in that part of the heart which never ceases to be a parent—no, not even in eternity.

But we stand on the shore.

We watch.

We cannot cry out to the independent pilot of his and her own ship. We haven't the right any more even to warn against treacherous waters, to shout how suicidal certain sea lanes are for children, when they become adults, take all rights unto themselves, just as Adam and Eve once chose for themselves and even God was silent then, watching then, knowing the consequences, ready to suffer the consequences with them, because he loved them; but saying nothing.

And so we pray to a God who knows our parental heart.

And if we scream, it is an interior anguish.

That is to say, we pray.

And this is what we pray:

O Lord, finally I know the terrible love with which you released your children into the world, because I feel that love for my child now. And I honor you. From my heart I honor you! I have but a few children; you had entire humankind.

When you had created them and provided them with everything they needed in the garden; when you had taught them their skills and their purposes in the world; when you had assured them of your good will, your protection, your abiding love—then you gave them the last and grandest, most dangerous gift of all. You gave them liberty. Independence— even from you.

What anxiety we suffer, watching the children go!

You gave them free will. The freedom to choose is freedom itself; but freedom cannot give the consequences away.

You said, "You may freely eat of every tree in the garden, but of one tree you shall not eat, lest you die."

You knew and you said it: *Lest they die.* In the highest

parental love you shared your knowledge with them and they were told: nothing was hidden from them. Nor, Lord, did you build a wall around this tree. You did not make eating impossible. You merely put your command and your love around it: *Don't! For your own good, don't!* And you left it up to them. They were free.

Likewise, now my children are free.

Moreover, they are free in a world not inclined to love—to love them or to love your commandments, either one. The world which doesn't love my children will lie to them as Satan (who does not love you) lied to your children. I love my children! But the world is nearer to them now than I am. The world shall have the greater power over them. But I love them! I love them! Always I suffer their consequences. I want them to be good for their *own* good; but if they are not, it is my stomach that suffers the punch with theirs, almost equal to theirs. But they don't know. All helplessly, I love them.

No! No, it is not finally a helpless love. You love them too, almighty God. And to you I make my cry, the pleading of a weak parent to The Strong One.

Dear, supernal Parent, God of my children, save them!

Even as you returned to the race which used its freedom selfishly, unto its death, even as you sent your only begotten Son to die the death which they deserved, return again and again to my young sons and my daughters, adults. In mercy, please! I fear for them if you do not.

Protect them against the enemies that would kill them. But if they must suffer storms or treachery, turn their suffering to advantage—that it always turn them back to you again.

O Lord, I am begging. I mean this prayer with all my heart.

Make my children humble. Let hurting cause in them a genuine humility. And let their transgressions cause no more harm than a personal hurt—for I know them. They will sin. And I beseech you: for their sinning do not damn them, do not let them die, but rather in hurting make them humble. And then, O merciful Father, accept this humility as repentance and let their repentance find your forgiveness and seize them thereby and hold them close unto your bosom forever and ever.

Save them from the world and from themselves. Amen. I love them, sweet Jesus. Amen.

Part IV

The Parent, Finally, of His Parents

25

Live Long on the Earth

The commandments have not expired. Nor have the holy promises that attend them been abolished.

When, therefore, I am asked regarding the future of some human community, some family, some nation— or the church, the visible church itself!—straightway I look for obedience to the commandments of God. Particularly I wonder regarding the one which urges honor for the parents: I look to see whether someone is singing songs to his aged mother—and if I can find him, I say, "The signs are good."

This is no joke. The best prognostication for the life of any community—whether it shall be long or short—is not financial, political, demographic, or even theological. It is moral. Ask not, "How strong is this nation?" nor "How many are they? How well organized? With what armies and resources?" Ask, rather: *How does this people behave?*

See, there is always set before us life and good or death and evil. If we walk in the ways of the sustaining God and obey his commandments, then we have chosen life—for the Lord *is* life and the length of any nation's days. This is flat practicality. How we *are* defines whether we shall continue to *be.*

Do we as a people honor our mothers and our fathers? Do we honor the generation that raised us—especially when it sinks down into an old and seemingly dishonorable age? When our parents twist and bow and begin to stink, what then? When they harden in crankiness, what then? Do we by esteeming them make them sweet and lovely again? The question is not irrelevant to our future, whether we shall have one or not. Its answer verily prophesies of *That it may be well with you and you may live long on the earth.*

The Hebrew word here translated *earth* may also be translated *land,* meaning more than just soil, meaning *country.* The promise attached to this commandment is precise: so long as the Israelites honored their parents, they would continue to live in the land that God had provided for them. If ever they began to neglect their parents or, worse, to scorn or in some way to hurt them, that break between the generations would break the people from their land as a sick tree breaks at the trunk and dies.

Even so we—as long as we sing to the mother who bore us the songs she heard in her youth, the same songs once she sang to us in lullaby—we may live long in the land.

I have seen the signs. In Wisconsin. In quiet obscurity, where I went to visit a friend of mine who lives with his mother in the farmhouse her father built one hundred years ago. She has a wasting disease. My friend cares for her.

M. is a studious man. In the evening he reads by a low lamp in the corner of the parlor. The light casts shadows on an ancient florid wallpaper, on heavy furniture, on the bed in the farther darkness where his mother sleeps. He reads through half-glasses, his head bent to the page, fingers at his chin. He reads very late because his mother may murmur softly—too softly to be heard from any other part of the house—and this is his signal to serve her.

But when he welcomed me to the farmhouse, it was daylight. He opened the door and grinned with thin lips his genuine pleasure at my coming and immediately invited me to the parlor.

The house smelled sweet and brown with cinnamon, tart with apples.

"Your mother's baking?" I asked as we walked.

"No," he said and ducked his head a bit, an angular apology. "No, she doesn't do that anymore."

"Then who—?"

"Oh, well," he said. Sheepish. "I see to the necessary things."

We entered the parlor, and so I understood.

His mother was sitting up in bed, a shawl around her shoulders, smiling. I, too, smiled and walked toward her. But M. interposed, introducing us with a formal civility as if the woman were very rich, as if we had never met before: "Mother, be pleased to meet—"

In fact, I've known M.'s mother almost as long as I have known him. But now it became clear that she had ceased to know me, and I was startled by the change. Her face was round, slack, soft, white, and, except for the querulous smile, expressionless. My dear old friend who once wore an apron and cooked for me, her face had the glaze of a dinner plate. Her watery glance never found my eyes but dribbled down my chest to my hands as if she were a child looking for candy.

M. said, "Shake hands with mother."

I did. As I reached, her right arm rose spontaneously. I took the powder-white hand that hung at the wrist and squeezed something like dough. She never ceased to smile, but questioningly. I stepped back. M. offered her a prune from a dish. She had a wonderful set of teeth. She was munching when we left the room.

We talked the rest of the day, M. and I. We strolled a sharp autumn countryside as the sun descended and the chill came down and the air smelled of crushable things, husks and hulls and leaves and the scented fires that burn them.

All the farmland had been sold, except five acres and the house itself. They kept a small orchard—and that was floating on the cool air too, a winey aroma.

I have always enjoyed the probing intellect of my friend's conversation: soft-spoken, forever undismayed, M. has a natural savvy which he has enriched with his reading. He could, if they would listen, counsel presidents.

Finally it was the night. I praised his apple pie and retired to my room and lay down and slept.

I tell you the truth—that very night I saw the signs:

At two in the morning I was awakened by a cry. I felt my stomach contract. I thought I heard a cat in the house, a lingering, feline wailing, inarticulate and mournful. It was a sort of screamed lamentation.

It seemed that someone was terribly hurt.

So I rose and followed the sound downstairs—through the kitchen to the parlor. A low lamp was lit. I peeped in.

This was no cat. This was M.'s mother. Her head was thrown backward, her mouth enormous, all her upper jaw and teeth in view. She was yowling: *Ya-ya-ya-na-naaaaah!*

M. himself was crouched at her bedside with a pan of water and cloths. He turned and saw me in the doorway. He smiled and motioned me to sit. I sat in his chair, under his reading lamp, granting them the privacy of darkness—but by the odor in the room I know what my friend was doing.

He was honoring his mother, exactly as the Lord God commanded.

He was washing away the waste. He was changing her diapers.

And he was singing to her.

Softly, in his mother's tongue, he was singing, *Müde bin ich, geh zu ruh*— Lullabies. The simple, sacred, everlasting songs.

And she was singing with him. That was the sound I had been hearing: no lamentation, no hurt nor sorrow, but an elderly woman singing with outrageous pleasure at the top of her lungs.

And lo: This old face was alive again. This old woman was as young as the child who first heard the lullaby, innocent, happy, wholly consoled. This old mother of my friend was dwelling in the music of her childhood. This was the face of one beloved, whose son obeyed the covenants and honored her—and kept her honorable thereby.

This boisterous singer is my sign. And the sign is good. Shall we endure? So long as such obedience continues among us, O my people, yes, it may be well with us. We may live long on the earth.

26

Red, Red, the Bloodred Kiss

*T*wo weeks ago I sat in the crowded holding area at one of the gates of Houston's Intercontinental Airport, waiting to board my flight home. First dribblingly, and then wondrously in so public a place, laughter rose up by the door of the jetway. It became a loud, footstomping hoot.

I glanced up.

Two young women were rooting through the enormous purse of a third, an older bonier woman who was obviously nervous, obviously the traveler of the three.

"Where you *got* them Tums?" cried a younger woman, her face and her full right arm deep inside this purse. "You know you need—*Whoop!*" she shrieked. "Lookee here!"

Laughing, laughing till tears streamed from her eyes, she drew forth and held up five magazines, a sandwich wrapped in wax paper, earplugs, small cans of juice, an umbrella—and a new package of underwear entitled: *Three Briefs.*

"Mamma!" she cried. "Oh, Mamma, what you want with

these?" The older woman looked baffled. The younger one laughed with a flashing affection. "You got plans you ain't tol' us about?" Maybe the two young women were daughters of their more solemn elder, maybe her granddaughters. "Honey, it's the Tums'll do you most good." She dived into the purse again. "Now where you got ... Oh, Mamma. Oh, Mamma," she whispered with suddenly softer wonder: "Look."

This young woman had a magnificent expanse of hip and the freedom of spirit to cover it in a bright red skirt, tight at the waist, wide behind, and tight again at the knee. She stood on spiky heels. Fashion forced her to walk by short wobbly steps, oddly opposite her amplitude of hip and cheek and laughter.

"Oh, Mamma!" Suffused with gentleness, she pulled from the purse a worn leather-bound Testament and Psalms. "Mamma, what? What you thinkin'?" The two women exchanged a silent look, each full of the knowledge of the other. The generations did not divide them.

"Well," said the older, bony woman, "you found the nourishment, but you ain't found the Tums." With a bark of laughter, Young Woman in Red hunkered down into the purse again—tottering on her tiny heels.

At the same time there came down the concourse an old man so gaunt in his jaw as to be toothless, bald and blotched on his skull, meatless arm and thigh. He sat in a wheelchair, listing to the right. The chair was being pushed through the crowds at high speeds by an attendant utterly oblivious of this wispy, thin, and ancient passenger.

The old man's eyes were troubled, but his mouth, sucked inward, was mute. His nose gave him the appearance of a hawk caught in a trap, helpless and resigned.

Now the attendant turned into our gate area, jerked the chair to a stop (bouncing the skeletal soul therein), reached down to set the brake, turned on his heel, and left.

But the brake was not altogether set, nor had the chair altogether stopped. It was creeping by degrees toward the generous hips of the woman whose face was buried in the generous purse of her elder, giggling.

The old man's eyes—the closer he rolled to this red rear end as wide as Texas—widened. He opened his mouth. He began to raise a claw. He croaked. And then he ran straight into the back of her knees.

Yow! Up flew the great purse, vomiting contents. Backward stumbled the young woman, a great disaster descending upon a crushable old man.

At the last instant, she whirled around and caught herself upon the armrests of the wheelchair, a hand to each rest. Her face froze one inch from the face of an astonished octogenarian. They stared at one another, so suddenly and intimately close that they must have felt the heat—each must have smelled the odor of the other.

All at once the woman beamed. "Oh, honey!" she cried. "You somethin' handsome, ain't you?" She leaned the last inch forward and kissed him a noisy smack in the center of his bald head. "I didn't hurt you none, did I?"

Strangers were strangers no longer. Suddenly they were something more.

Slowly there spread over the features of this ghostly old man the most beatific smile. Oh, glory and heat and blood and love rose up in a body dried to tinder.

And the young woman burst into thunderous laughter. "Look at you!" she bellowed. "What yo wife gon' say when she see my lipstick kiss on yo head? Ha ha ha!" He reached to touch the red, and she cried, "You gon' have some explainin' to do!"

That old man closed his eyes in soundless laughter with the woman—two made one for a fleeting moment.

So did the elderly woman, who still hadn't found her Tums, laugh.

So did I, surprising myself. So did a host of travelers who had been watching the episode with me. We all laughed, gratefully. *We,* in the brief event and the silly joke of wives and kisses, were unified.

It wasn't the joke, of course. It was goodwill. It was spontaneous affection. It was the willingness of a single woman, wholly human even in the public eye—in risk and under judgment—suddenly, swiftly to love another, to honor him, to give him something graceful without hesitation or fear, something free and sweet and durable. But she gave it to us all. I won't forget her. I beg God, in such revealing moments, that I might be as generous and good as she.

There was a sanctity in the kiss of that woman.

And in this: that the man was as white as the snows of Sweden, and the woman as black as the balmy nights of Africa.

27

Dorothy—
In the Crown of God

One summer we took Dorothy to the mountains. It was a risk, but it had become necessary to initiate certain changes in her life.

Soft Dorothy was as citified as they come, though the city she comes from is tiny. She had lived her whole life in the shelter of her parents, who kept that life very regular: sleeping, rising, eating, a little work, a load of ease, and ice cream before she went to bed each night. Almost nothing interrupted the daily round of Dorothy-affairs. She never got caught in the rain downtown. She seldom *walked* to town. She rode everywhere. She had almost never been separated from her parents.

But her father was eighty-nine years old, her mother not much younger—and Dorothy herself was forty. The clock which ticked her day so neatly was likewise ticking the lives of her parents to their ends. It was time that she should experience a real separation from them before death forced the issue and sorrow complicated everything. So we took her with us to the mountains.

But it was a risk.

Round Dorothy was ever exceedingly private. She squirreled money in secret places in her room. More valuable than money were the pictures she clipped from magazines, pictures she hid so well they shan't be found till doomsday. Her eyes would open wide with panic when little children entered her bedroom. Who can control little children? But even then Dorothy said almost nothing. She was private. She buried her thoughts; she muted her basic communication in grunts and grumbles. But she didn't have to talk, after all. Her mother knew her needs, decided her desires, spoke for her—spoke, indeed, even before Dorothy thought she had a thought. It really was time, you see, for Dorothy to step out on her own.

But round Dorothy was also exceedingly—round. The woman stood no higher than my elbow, yet was wider than I am by half at the beam. Cute little ankles, prodigious thighs, and a body as round as a medicine ball. To the *mountains* with Dorothy? Why, she could scarcely climb the stair steps one flight up.

Her eyes are slant behind their glasses; her tongue lolls on the lower lip; her chins redouble backward; her expression is generally benign and vague.

Dorothy has Down's syndrome. She is what people call "retarded." She is also Thanne's sister, my sister-in-law; and since I was to teach for several weeks at Holden Village in the Cascade Mountains of the Northwest, we took Hob in our hands and said: "Let Dorothy come with us."

Her mother swallowed painfully, considered the need, wept with a mother's solicitude, and relented. She packed for her daughter a suitcase the size of Montana (in which *she* squirreled handwritten instructions not shorter than the Book of Leviticus. For example: "Dorothy's bazooka is in her underwear. She likes to play it." Her *bazooka*? What was that? Ah, when we looked in her underwear we found her *kazoo*).

O Holden Village, hold your breath!—here comes Dorothy, the daughter of her mother. Holden, be patient and kind. We can all sacrifice a little to train this woman-child in independence, right?

Oh, and Holden? Please give us rooms low down, on a flat level with the rest of your buildings, because Dorothy is so very . . . round.

So we went to the wilds, the Wangerins six and sister Dorothy of the wide, wide eyes. It was an airplane flight from Chicago to Seattle, a car trip to the town of Chelan, a boat trip for three hours up the lake while mountains rose around us to dangerous sizes, and finally a bus trip up those mountains— miles high in the mighty, remote, foredooming mountains of God.

In Holden Village, then, Dorothy rolled her beanbag body off the bus, looked up at the craggy peaks yet higher than she, patted her bosom, and sighed: "Whew!"

The registrar met us. He pointed to our quarters. He pointed upward at an angle of forty degrees, to the top of a long road. *Whew!* We—all seven of us—bowed our heads and climbed.

"Whew!" said Dorothy. She moved as slowly as the moon. *Whew!* This medicine ball expressed herself in a variety of sighs, one for each new height as she struggled upward. And when we achieved the top of the hill—when still we stood at the bottom of the staircase that extended up to the front porch of our house—Dorothy stopped and produced a truly admirable cavalcade of sighs: "Whew! Whew! Whew!"— fanning her face, popping her eyes, and grinning. Grinning! She was Rocky Balboa at the end of his run.

Now I declare to you a wonder: Dorothy was not mute at all! She was profoundly expressive to those who had the ears to hear her.

Later, when she spied the busy ground squirrels, she paused and offered them a series of happy squeal-sighs, as if meeting with glee some long-lost relatives. When deer raised their noble necks and gazed at this round dollop of a woman, she honored them with murmurous sacred sighs as soft as lullabies. When she stepped on a slat bridge over roaring waters—which water we could see between the boards below our feet—she made a bleating sigh, and I realized how brave she was to stand so near the tumbling chaos. And when she lifted her eyes to the ring of mountains around us, and when she grew gravely still, allowing one long sigh, one eternal expulsion of breath to escape her languorous throat, I said in my soul: *Listen, my sister is praying!*

Retarded? Who is the fool that says so? This woman had an apprehension of the universe more intimate and more devout than my own. Her knowing was not troubled by extraneous thought. Dorothy had a language of genuine sophistication and of immediate response. Sighs were her words. Add to that some simple English grunts which even I could understand, and Dorothy was bilingual.

I had been to Holden Village three times before that summer, but I had never seen so well the crown surrounding it, had never seen with primal eyes until I stood with Dorothy looking up and sighing. I took squirrels to my heart, honored deer, and praised the God of supernal peaks—because of Dorothy. She was the quick one. My responses were baffled and slow. She was the one who trained me, both in seeing and in speaking. I, in the high, green tiara of the Deity—I, in simple creation—was the retarded one. How often we get it backward. How much we miss when we do!

On the second night we were there, Dorothy went up on her toes and embraced me in a mighty hug and kissed my chin and murmured, "Whew!"

I, too, said, "Whew!"

Her word meant, "What a good day!"

Mine meant, *Thank you, sweet sister, for taking me to the mountains this summer.*

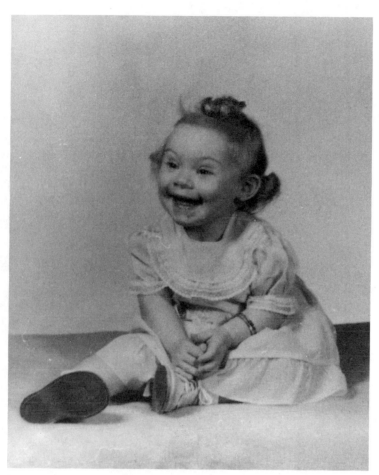

Dorothy Bohlmann

28

Fishing, My Friend and I

I used to fish with Arthur Bias before he died. I think of those days now, and I wonder: Do the days pass away with the person?

I mean: Those days were warm and peaceful and free of enmity. If anyone was mad at me, I didn't know it. Arthur liked me. "Rev?" he said. "Reverent, y'wanna toss a line t'mornin'?" But he died, and the days have changed since then.

Now there's a whole load of folk most mad and most particular that I should know it—a frownin' shoal of folk, a letter-writin', telephone-callin', grudge-and-memory-bearin' rudeness of furious folk.

Well, I've acquired a notoriety neither Arthur nor I could ever have imagined in those sweeter days, as well as a publicity neither of us would have wanted. That's one thing changed, yes. And Arthur died in the 1970s. That's another thing. And I haven't been fishing lately. There's the third. Maybe the fault lies in one of them.

Or what do you think?—maybe the world is angrier now than it used to be? Maybe the world is lookin' for doorsteps to dump the grumpiness on—and the handiest porch gets the pile, and I, by my writing, am handy?

Are people less content? Quicker to take offense? Slower to forgive? Certain that those whose opinions differ are not just different but are *enemies,* are wicked people deserving attack and revilement and public punishment?

What happened to plain happiness?

I miss you, Arthur Bias.

Old man, enormous man, deep-voiced, large-jowled, slow-striding black man: you were a police officer in your day. That was—Oh, my!—that was back in the '40s, the '50s and the '60s. I came to know you after you had retired. But you hadn't retired the stories. You told them while we fished, your eyes gone thin with remembering, squinting toward Kentucky, talking and talking in tones that knew no guile nor anger.

You bottom-fished. Therefore, we both bottom-fished. Took less energy letting a line hang down from its red-and-white bobber, a grub on the point of the hook. Or an angle worm. Or a cricket. Caught catfish on bacon fat. Bullhead on cheese. Carp on anything.

Tossed the line. Sat down in a lawn chair. Lit a pipe. Slit the eye. Stayed silent a long while. Let the droning flies soften our brains to drowsiness. Sighed at the goodness of an uncomplicated world. Thanked God for lazy afternoons. Dozed.

You would doze, Arthur, making moist buzzings in your cavernous nose. But then you'd wake to the tug of a fish, twitch your brows, reel it in, and start a story, all at once.

Old man, I miss the benediction of your presence, your life constructed of common things. You desired no more than that. Ah, but you were *more* than contented: You were *kind.*

"Ahmmmmm," you'd murmur in the vast passages of that nose. "Never did pull mah service revolver more than a few times, nope. Never had to. Made mah wishes known in other ways."

You had walked a beat in the black center of our city. Could make your leather heels crack that sidewalk. And you knew the people, the renters and the owners, the houses and the projects—knew them by name. (*Crack! Crack!*) Knew them from babies at they's mamma's knee. You could use a moral persuasion. After that, the authority of your massive size. And then intimacy. Then the badge. But the gun—that vomit of wrath and death—was the last persuasion of all for you.

"Tell you wot," you said, squinting across the Ohio River toward sunshine and Kentucky, "even them long-legged boys and them gum-snappin' girls'ud heed me—on account of I knew they's mammas. Ahmmmmm, ha-ha, oh yeah! Hoo! Mamma'ud willow-switch 'em, if'n I asked as much, 'cause she an' me been singin' in the church choir since we was chirren.

"Well, an' I didn' care none if they liked me or no. But I'll tell you wot." You leaned back and tipped an old face to the sunlight and smiled. "They liked me."

Arthur, you made that lawn chair bulge both backward and bottomward. You made a neighborhood civil—*Crack! Crack!* You took the tough job and turned it to kindness. When you laughed, heaving your shoulders and stomach in seismic displacement, I felt the earth respond.

And when you lay dying in Deaconness Hospital, you asked for green beans. You talked of the exact right way to cook green beans, in a bit o' bacon fat, with sausages boiled to the point of popping. You tol' me 'bout suckin' the soft white meat straight off the catfish bones. You grinned, old man, in the deep pillows of your bed and spoke of food with as much fervor as ever you spoke of the law, or of your beat, or of your wife. It was all one with you, and all of it sufficient. That which you had, you cherished. That which you did not have, you did not desire. Therefore, an afternoon at the edge of a sleepy water was no less than Eden prepared by God especially for you. And for me, whom you invited along in easy company.

I miss you, Arthur Bias!

I miss Eden.

I miss the unspoken conviction that people, despite their differences, are worthy of honor and latitude, if not of downright affection. I miss a lawman given to mercy. I miss the perfect assurance that fishing's enough, that this afternoon's sunlight is surely enough. And I wonder what caused the change among us. What did you take away? What did your whole generation take away with you when you died?

Why is this present people so quick to rebuke? Why is anger faster and fiercer than gratitude or praise? Why (for instance) does a writer generate more mail from mad folks (who take things so personally) than from the peaceful ones whose word is by nature good will and welcome?

Oh, Arthur, maybe the world has not changed. Maybe you were, in your ordinariness, extraordinary—a cop who caused harmony! A friend who, in fishing, hooked God at the heart. A man of strength and love together. A man of law but not of condemnation. Law does not require condemnation, does it?

But grace requires kindness, doesn't it?

And grace is this, that an old black man took a young white pastor to his bosom and told him stories and redeemed the time with kindness.

I miss you. I yearn the kindness of common people. It seems so uncommon a quality lately—

29

Rise, Dorothy, Rise

*G*enuine love is defined by this, that it is prepared to sacrifice itself for the sake of the beloved.

Sham love, on the other hand, makes *itself* the motive, the cause and the end of relationship. Sham love may know "sacrifice," but only as a means to reach some goal of its own. It says, "Since I have given up so much for you, now you owe me . . ." There is no giving without some getting, even if that which is gotten is merely public praise or the sweet internal feeling: *What a good person am I!*

Genuine love serves. Neither requiring nor expecting something in return. Its character is, simply, to serve—and those who stumble against these twin axioms of sacrifice and service will likewise stumble against the cross. They will fall down crying, "Scandal!"

Sham love stumbles.

Sham love may *think* it desires to serve the beloved; in fact, it desires only (and precisely) the beloved for itself. It desires his company, her person—some respondent love. So its service is not an end in itself. Sham love may perform the most difficult services, things its beloved shall absolutely need—until she becomes dependent upon them and thereby bound unto her "servant," her benefactor. Do you see? Sham love fulfills itself in the end by possessing the other.

Genuine love has one goal only: the health and honor, the full flowering and the *freedom* of the beloved. It serves her that she might become her own most beautiful self. It seeks the rose within the bud, and then—when all the world sees but a nubble—it nourishes that bud with rain and the richness of its own self. This is holy sacrifice, the outpouring of one self upon another, until that other opens up and blossoms. Genuine love rejoices when the beloved is finally lovely and perfectly free.

Sham love never perceives the image intrinsic within the other. Rather, it makes up its own image of what she ought to be according to its own designs, then imposes this fiction upon her. When she does not conform (well, she can't: she is *herself,* not *his* self) sham love might remain resolutely blind to what she is and pretend that *she* has conformed, imprisoning her within its restrictive lie. Or else it will blame her for the failure: "I'm so disappointed in you!" Thus justified, sham love will try harder to force conformity, or will reject her altogether. In either case, it confesses no wrong. It believes it has *been* wronged.

One of the plainest signs of sham love is self-pity.

Another is fear of freedom.

Since the goal of sham love is itself, it must control the beloved. In fact, it measures her love by the amount of obedience she gives its will. Therefore, though genuine love takes a genuine joy in the free flight of the beloved, sham love is angered by her slightest act of independence; angered first, then threatened; then frightened by the independence that bodes separation; and finally, if she has flown indeed, sham love falls into the despair of the unfulfilled.

Listen to the songs of the world and the language it uses for love. How often the point of the song is the singer! Listen to the wisdom of the world: "Feeling good about myself, yeah!

Satisfaction is my birthright, and my worth you must acknowledge, just because I AM." Such a demand—though it makes a worldly sense—is exactly the opposite of sacred love, for it makes a god of the self.

It must always be offended by the cross.

But listen, and I will show you a more excellent way.

More than forty years ago my parents-in-law brought Dorothy into the world—their thirteenth child, an infant afflicted with Down's syndrome. Because of her mental incapacity, they chose to keep her at home; and though she learned much and went forth to work each day, they lavished upon her more service than any other child required. In fact, her presence and her need required her parents to continue *as* parents long after they might have been taking their ease. Martin added ninety years to his age and still was parenting a child; Gertrude added eighty-four. But this is love, that they served with unceasing, uncomplaining devotion for forty-one years.

But this, too, is genuine love: that finally they had to stop serving her.

Dorothy has moved into a group home established for the mentally handicapped. She received her own room, her own place in life. She picked out her own wallpaper and curtains—and all this was pure delight to her. She was free.

But her mother was weeping. And her father, full of love, was solemn. Suddenly they weren't parents any more. They were not needed as they had been. They had sacrificed, for their daughter's sake, their significant reason to *be*, had sacrificed something of their own identities. This is love. The emptiness of the house; the release of its sometime sweet inhabitant, who had been life and focus for old eyes; the farewell of the heart: "Goodbye, goodbye, Dorothy"—this is love.

But Gertrude and Martin knew how close they were to dying. They knew that Dorothy would suffer a double trauma should they die while she was still beside them, since any new home would then be ruined by the reason for going and the grieving that brought her there. So Gertrude and Martin chose to bear the grief of departure themselves, while Dorothy could feel a full, untroubled joy in it. This is a gift she may never comprehend. This is her parents' personal sacrifice. This is love.

Just before she was driven away, they kissed her. Martin moved slowly in a walker. Gertrude, for a weak heart, puffed small puffs of air. Dorothy clambered into the car without a second thought, grinned, and waved brightly. Gertrude rushed back into the house, embarrassed by her tears. Martin bent into the car window. "Be good," the old man whispered. "Be good, Dorothy. Good-bye."

And then he, too, wept.

But he let her go. The bud was becoming a rose. The rains that washed and watered her may never see this blossom blow. They serve, and then they sink into the earth. This is a genuine love.

30

Will the Circle Be Unbroken

*I*t occurs to me precisely now that the difference between giving gifts to one's children and giving gifts to one's parents is fundamental.

Gifts are meant to delight our children. To give glee and laughter, the fun of sensation. Discovery. Games.

Or if the gift must be some useful thing, then it's meant to educate the kid, to train or nourish or clothe or keep her. In either case, as much as we may love to give them, gifts to the child come of a parent's duty. They come of love, too, certainly; but *we* choose. We decide what's best—or else what's permissible. And so we ought. It is our business to care for our children, and gifts are one element of that responsibility.

But gifts are meant to *honor* our parents.

We give to our children fresh. We give them things they've never considered giving us. As parents we initiate the process—hoping they get the idea, of course, that selflessness and kindness and concern for others are all good things, worthy of imitation; and so do we continue to teach them even when we give them things they do not need, things for their delight.

But to parents we give *back*.

They are the ones who initiated the giving long ago by giving first to us. In fact, they will likely *need* nothing we might give them. (Necessary care for a helpless old age is another matter, not so much the giving of a gift as, again, our proper duty; for then we are parents for the second time and they for the second time are children.) And if they do not need the thing we give them (for their education or their nourishment) then it is the giving itself which is significant. The gesture.

It is *thanks*-giving.

It is a remembering of all things past.

It is closure to a love which they began, a solemn and holy circle.

It is, therefore, wholeness to a relationship: parenthood's and childhood's perfect health.

It is that sweetest of commandments (one of only two which do not say *don't*, but *do*): Do "honor your father and your mother that it may be well with you and you may live long in the land."

It is the commandment which need not threaten nor persuade, the commandment which arises from our own heart's desire when all is already well with us because our parents saw to it in the first place.

It is honor.

Giving gifts to our parents is meant to honor them. It declares them honorable. It acknowledges by a visible act their worth. It enshrines *them*. *They* are revealed as the finest gift first given by God unto us, their children; and their earlier kindness now is elevated before ourselves and our community. "Lo," says the giving of this gift, "how important these people are; how important they have been!"

This Christmas Thanne and I will, as we have for twenty-two years, choose presents for our four children—carefully, extravagantly, parentally. And it will gladden our hearts to gladden theirs.

But just last month I was able to send my father a book dedicated to him, to him alone. I entitled the book after the psalmist's words, *Mourning into Dancing,* because it describes the marvelous power of God to move us from sorrow to joy again. But I dedicated it to my father because he was himself the source, you see, of much of my knowledge: whose gifts to me were teaching, training, education, whose gifts were given first.

So with the book I sent him a letter written in my own delight. I told him that my book was his book. I declared that its contents came first from him, the insights, the theology, the learning, the experience, the stories. He, I said, had modeled before me the faith that imbued my book. Oh, yes, the greatest gift he gave me (I wrote) was faith itself! For in my earthly father this child observed a perfect trust in his heavenly Father—and the Father of my father is mine as well.

I wrote: "Dad, I am only just giving *back* your book to you. Your son is celebrating *your* spirit and *your* wisdom and *your* love. He is your mirror."

I wrote that my dedication is the truth: *For my father, my senior forever.*

I wrote that my book is a public, perpetual memorial to him, published in his honor.

Something has come to completion, don't you see? And I have, by honoring my father, received a benefit beyond my expectation and my deserving: I view the world from standing on my Daddy's shoulders, a lofty promontory.

But more than that: yesterday I received from him a letter too, a letter so grand and good that it echoed down four generations. Dad recalled his own grandfather, a pastor in rural Illinois with whom a little boy rode in horse-drawn buggies to visit parishioners long ago; he recalled his father, the first Walter of three, a pastor too, who ordained his son, my father, also into the ministry; he spoke of his own service unto God. And then of mine. He lifted our mothers, our grandmothers, and our great-grandmothers on high, like candles that shed light upon them they loved. His letter gave me place within the long train of holy witnesses, my forebears; and simply, simply it revealed my father as the singer of these.

By giving him honor, I called forth from him that deep, long song in which we all finally find rest, nestling within our families, the ancestors past, the people present, the descendants yet to come.

My father sang, and I saw us both well met together: Wangerins. It is well.

Ah, yes, we *shall* live long on the earth.

Know, then dear friends of mine, the profound importance and the celestial rightness of giving gifts to your parents.

Or why did God think it significant enough to make it one of but ten commandments?

It is in such honoring that nations survive and do not die.

Only insofar as we honor our parents shall our children have place in the world. And then theirs. It is a living circle.

And that is a promise.

31

My Name Is Dorothy Bohlmann

*D*ear Dorothy:

Just last Saturday we gathered at Mom and Dad Bohlmann's to celebrate Independence Day. You came—you and all your mates from group home, both the staff and the "handicapped" inhabitants. Thanne and I were there too, of course, with four other Bohlmann "children" and their spouses. They all have spouses. All your mother's children married—except two. Of the fourteen children she bore, only two did not leave home to marry and to bear children of their own. But Raymond died when he was an infant, more than half a century ago.

And you have Down's syndrome.

Dorothy, did you ever stop enjoying the weddings of your many siblings? Did you ever think it was your turn to be given such attention, such a beautiful day, and such a good good-bye? And then did it ever seem that the ceremony everyone else received had been denied to you alone? The last child to leave left nearly twenty years ago. But you stayed. Did you watch and wait in yearning? Did yearning ever turn to envy, and envy into sorrow?

It is my instinct that you did. I think you, too, in the natural course of growing older, wanted to marry. It's only an instinct. You never spoke. For years and years you made your feelings known in tears or smiles or fussy grunts—or sighs. You said "Whew" a thousand ways. But no words.

Well, and it is also my instinct that having been granted no choice in something so universally human, you exercised choice in one of the few areas over which no one had control but you. You could not choose not to eat, of course. And your mother insisted on choosing *what* you ate, *what* you wore, *where* you went, *how* you got there, *when* you would come home. I think you marked off a tiny area of independence by withdrawing into silence. No one could reach you there.

Dorothy, I think there was a part of you that *chose* not to talk.

So, on the Fourth of July last week, we "normal" folks stood on the library lawn in Watseka, Illinois, and watched a parade in which the whole town participated. Your house-mates dressed like clowns and strode the street with great solemnity, staring straight ahead—oh, so obedient and so earnest!

Then we gathered in Mom's backyard under a splendid blue midwestern sky. We gave thanks to God for independence and for freedom. We sang "God Bless America." We prayed. We ate. You sat in state, it seemed to me, receiving the attentions of many friends, the only one related to everyone there—and then it dawned on me how you are the hinge that joins two families, for you are a Bohlmann, and you are the only Bohlmann in the group home. If the Wangerins and the Bohlmanns had gathered, then Thanne would have been the hinge between two families because she married me.

Because she left her home and I left mine and we made a new home together, joining two.

I gazed long at you that afternoon, dear sister, and I said in my soul, *No, but Dorothy did leave her mother and her father to cleave unto others, and they have made a new home together—*

Oh, Dorothy, how you have changed!

Look at you, Lady: here comes Donny of the group home, whizzing through the yard (Donny, whose face is as aerodynamic as a 747, is always whizzing); he suddenly stops to hug you and ask how you are doing, seriously searches your eyes for a whole second, then is seized with another spasm of speed, and whizzes on. Donny wears an old World-War-One-flying-ace hat with earflaps. And you? You accept his adoration as something natural to him and due to you. Then you happen to catch me watching you. So you wave a little wind into your face and you smile back at me and you sigh, "Whew, whew!"—as if to say, *That's Donny. He'll take your breath away.*

Do you remember when we went to the mountains together? That was four years ago. You still make the silly sigh you made then, but you scarcely *need* to any more. You've lost roundness! Motion is easier now than before. The new home which you have made with others has made you a healthier woman. Independence. I said in my soul, *No, Dorothy's no different from any child of Gertrude after all.* Independence is the beginning of health, an absolutely necessary thing.

Yet Gertrude suffered when you left her. That was two years ago. And since you were the last to leave of her fourteen, it was, I believe, as if all fourteen symbolically left with you; motherhood itself departed Gertrude when you did. How long did it take her to reconcile herself? She kept appearing in your new home, still making decisions for you, rearranging your clothes in the dresser drawers, still instructing you in what to wear. Well, and then you made silence your privacy: you thrust out your lip and folded your arms, and sometimes you wore exactly what you wanted to wear, though it wounded and outraged your poor mother. For something so wrong as this, someone must be at fault. Well, so she'd blame the staff of the group home for letting you get away with murder. Well, so everyone was upset for a while. Independence is a terrible thing. It tears from those who are left behind their very reason for being. It causes a nearly catastrophic loneliness. It was very hard on Mom. Recently I wrote that she has stopped crying about your absence. She wrote back straightway to tell me I was wrong. She still cries.

She's eighty-seven this year. What a change she had to sustain in her old age! Her heart is weak, this mother of many, this grandmother of multitudes. It cannot be long before she and Martin shall die. They know that. They speak of it, not always peacefully but always, always faithfully. She trembles when she moves too much. Martin is ninety-two. He drags a walker slowly. He had to lean on his son's arm in order to come down the porch stairs into the yard for our Independence Day picnic, and there he sat in a wheelchair making jokes. Both of your parents have minds as lucid as your own heart is lucid, Dorothy. Yes, Gertrude still cries for you. Perhaps she always will. And I think you know that, don't you?

I watched you throughout the length of a long, lazy afternoon. And before the midwestern sun had set, sweet sister, I saw you do two marvelous things.

One was new and astonishing. It took my breath away. It made me know how much you've grown and how good "marriage" has been for you. The other was natural unto you, no change at all, the same sort of thing you've been doing all your life but no less marvelous for that.

In the midst of the day's activity, I heard something. I heard you. Under the noises of your housemates, who speak a yowling sort of English, who laugh with perfect delight and lolling tongues, who rush hither and yon as if accomplishing some business so urgent the sky would fall without it; under the hubbub of eating and gossip and fire-cracking, the dashing of the children; under the long, slow snoozing of the sun, I heard a murmuring. I looked and saw that your spirit had withdrawn into its private vale, and I thought that the day had become too much for you again. But then I saw your lips move. You were repeating the same soft sentence over and over.

Dorothy, you were speaking! Sister, you were talking— although you seemed oblivious of the loud celebration all around you: talking to yourself, then.

Well, I crept near you to hear you the better but slowly, slowly, so that my coming would not disturb the moment nor destroy the quiet sentence. And then it was you who took my breath away.

With your head bent as if contemplating some complicated thing, gazing into your two palms upturned in your lap, scarcely moving your lips, you were murmuring, "My name is Dorothy Bohlmann. My name is Dorothy Bohlmann. My name is Dorothy Bohlmann—"

I said in my soul, *This woman is free! This woman is whole! No, she is in nothing diminished. She is the equal of any child of Gertrude and Martin, the peer of any child of God.*

Thirteen children indeed did leave to make new homes for themselves and new lives, too. Only Raymond did not. You did. The only difference between you and your siblings is that you were the last to go and bore the greater burden therefore. But now you, Dorothy, are fully adult. Let no one lisp when they speak to you. Let no one simplify speech and exaggerate their tone as if they were talking to a child of small understanding. In that sense you are no child at all.

And in another sense you are more mature than most of my acquaintances.

Near the end of the day, after the rest of the group home had departed, leaving you with us for the night, after the yard had been cleaned and while we sat chatting, entering evening, suddenly Mom cried out in pain and grabbed her leg. All her children rushed toward her. "No!" she said, waving people back and trying to laugh the pain away, but it kept returning in stabs and she couldn't help crying out again: "Oh! *Oh, NO!*"

It had been a hard day. Mom doesn't know how to quit. Moreover the party had been her idea. She wanted to make some gesture of thanksgiving to the staff of the group home. She wanted somehow to say that she didn't blame them any more. Gertrude is making peace. Your mother, Dorothy, is laboring to let you go. I think she is granting you your liberty. It was a day made hard, then, as much by the work of the heart as of the body.

"*Ow!*" she cried. Tears broke down her cheeks.

Immediately your face twisted with anxiety. You felt your mother's pain. It is your skill immediately to enter another soul and to feel precisely what that one feels.

And you love your mother.

Gertrude allowed Thanne to come near her. It was a severe muscle spasm in her leg; it wanted a hard massage. And you. You crept near your mother, too, patting and patting her leg with your small hand, you and Thanne, sisters side by side: where Thanne's hands went your hand followed, your eyes deep within your mother's eyes—and that, Dorothy, is as marvelous as anything you've ever done, because of the unsullied love it revealed, but then it is exactly what you have done all your life. It is natural to you. Independence has not changed sympathy. Independence does not cancel love. It transfigures it, making it purely a gift.

So your touch eased your mother like a medicine.

And I said in my soul, *No, but Dorothy is different from us after all. She is better. She loves more quickly and with less confusion.*

Ah, Dorothy, I think God honors hearts more than brains. You are the image of God in my world. In you the best of the child continues, while the best of adulthood emerges. Your declaration of independence never stole a state nor severed a nation nor warred against another soul. It only allowed you to return love for love in greater measure than before.

I love you, my sister.

Walt

32

When You Get There, Wait!

*L*ittle one, are you afraid of the dark?

Is that why you grab my hand and press against me? Because you are frightened?

Well, if we were still in the city I would show you the places where good people live. I'd name them and describe their kindness. Then if we had trouble, we could walk to a door and knock and get help.

In the city I would tell you where the hospital is and how to avoid dark alleys and which streets are well-lit. Or else I would just take you home. . . .

But we're not in the city, are we? And dark is darker where no human lights are. Even the noises are foreign here: no human machinery, no cars, no trucks, no TV, or tapes, or radio.

Little one! You cling to my arm as though the touch itself will keep you from harm, as though I were a good strong guard; and yet you tremble!

Are you still so scared of the dark?

O sweetheart, if we were out in the country now I would teach you the goodness of God's creation, even at night. I'd show you the stars and tell you their tales till they became your friends: the giant Orion (three stars for his belt and three for his dagger), the seven sisters all in a bunch (called the Pleiades, even in Scripture), Cassiopeia (whose shape makes a bent W like my initial). I'd light the star of Bethlehem. I'd talk about the angels, "the hosts of heaven," until the night skies were crowded by kindly spirits and we were not lonely below them.

In the country I'd make you hear the wind; I'd teach you the breath of God therewith, the *spiritus Dei*. God, who made it, keeps it still. The Creator laughs at the bullfrog's burp and loves the mockingbird—melodies, melodies, all night long. The phantom flight of the owl, the cricket's chirrup, the wolf's exquisite, killing harmonies—all these you would hear as the handiwork of God, just as you yourself are God's good handiwork. And then, my dear, you would be consoled. . . .

But we're not in the country, are we?

Little one, you whimper with fear. You turn and you bury your face in my bosom. I hug you with all my strength, with all my love. I rock you and rock you and stroke your thin hair—but still you are scared of the dark.

O my dear heart! O my dear, if you were going blind, if *that* were the darkness into which you descended, I would teach you touching—and feeling itself would be your light.

I'd lift your fingers to my face and let you touch me from temple to chin. Brush my lashes. Brush my smiling eyes. Linger at my cheekbone. Take upon your fingertips my kisses. Then take my hand and let me walk you through the dark world till all its furniture becomes familiar to you.

But . . . but the blindness you suffer is worse than that, isn't it?

Baby, afraid of the dark! Scared of the prison the darkness shuts around you! Frightened because you are soon nowhere at all, in spaces invisible, endless, empty. . . .

O little one, we know what your darkness is, don't we?

It's old age. You have grown old. And now comes the deepest darkness of all: you are dying.

My little one, my darling! The dark is your departure. You are leaving this world altogether, going to that undiscovered country from whose bourn no traveler returns. Yes? Yes.

Yes, and my darkness is sorrow, because I must remain behind.

Hush, old hoary head. My best beloved, hush. Let me hold you a while. Cling to me as tightly as you please, and I will whisper the thoughts that occur to me now.

No. This is not some city through which we travel. Yet there is a city ahead of you. And you shall enter before I do. But I am coming, and then it shall be *you* who welcomes *me* and makes the streets of that place familiar to me.

Because you are dying in faith, my little one—you who always were but a pilgrim on this earth. You're finishing the trip begun by baptism; you are entering a better country, that is, a heavenly country. Wherefore God is not ashamed to be called your God—for he hath prepared for you this city!

And when you arrive, you won't need me to show you around. God will meet you there. Alleys and highways, God will show you everything—but first he'll take from your vision the crust of old age, the terrors and the troubles of this present world: for God himself shall wipe all tears from your eyes; and there shall be no more death neither sorrow, nor crying anymore.

And no: the dark surrounding you now is not the countryside either, nor sky nor stars nor the woofings and bleats of God's creatures. It is, in fact, their absence, since you are passing away from all this.

Ah, but you go from creation to its Creator! You go to the God who conceived of Eden and Paradise and everything between the two. Better than the handiwork of God, dear heart, is God himself.

But yes: dying is a kind of blindness. It is preparation for deeper sight and dearest insight. Little one, this darkness is not because you cannot see, but because the world cannot *be* seen. The material world is becoming a shadow before you, so that the coming world (bright with divine reality) may not blind you at your arrival. That city is brighter than sunlight. It hath no need of the sun in it. For the glory of God doth lighten it, and the Lamb is the light thereof.

Hush, now. Close your eyes. Don't be afraid. I'll hold you with my lowly love till God receives you in his highest, most holy love. My darling, you are embarking through darkness on your best adventure. Only the start is scary. The rest is endlessly marvelous, eternally beautiful.

But when you get there, wait!

Turn around. Look back through the glorious light, and watch for me. I am coming, too.

This and much else in this book
is for Gertrude and Martin Bohlmann, my parents-in-law,
whom I do so dearly love
W. W.

Gertrude Bohlmann   Martin Bohlmann